# Craft
# Design &
# Technology

——Edited by——
## RICHARD KIMBELL

——Authors——
## JOHN PLATER · TRISTRAM SHEPARD

——with contributions from——
## DAVE BARLEX · MIKE BYFORD · RICHARD KIMBELL

THAMES/HUTCHINSON

Thames Television's five year *Craft, Design and Technology* course for secondary schools is now available for educational use on video cassette.

It presents *Craft, Design and Technology* as an active subject and will motivate students to get involved by stimulating their interest in designing, making and evaluating. Many of the programmes are suitable for use with GCSE classes.

For further information on the programmes, or for a set of teacher's notes, please contact Non-Theatric Sales, Thames Television International,149 Tottenham Court Road, London W1P 9LL.

Photographs and ideas from the Thames Television series *Craft, Design and Technology* are referred to in the text of this book by the use of the Thames Television logo, as shown below.

Hutchinson Education

An imprint of Century Hutchinson Ltd
62-65 Chandos Place, London WC2N 4NW

Century Hutchinson Australia Pty Ltd
PO Box 496, 16-22 Church Street, Hawthorn, Victoria 3122, Australia

Century Hutchinson New Zealand Ltd
PO Box 40-086, Glenfield, Aukland 10, New Zealand

Century Hutchinson South Africa (Pty) Ltd Po Box 337, Bergvlei 2012, South Africa

First published 1987 by Hutchinson Education in association with Thames Television International Ltd, 149 Tottenham Court Road, London W1P 9LL

© Richard Kimbell and Thames Television 1987

Designed and illustrated by The Pen and Ink Book Co Ltd
Printed and bound in Great Britain by Scotprint, Musselburgh

ISBN 0 09 172461 9

# CONTENTS

# Acknowledgements

We would like to thank the following for their kind permission to reproduce photographs and illustrations:

John Riley (page 6); John Riley, Secondary Examinations Council (page 7); Justin Munroe, Caroline Zianian (page 8); David Eberlin, Tony Stone Worldwide (page 9); John Riley (page 11); Eurotunnel (page 12); John Cave (page 15); Secondary Examinations Council (page 16); Justin Munroe (page 17); Andrew Breckon/Andrew Morgan (page 18); Barnaby's Picture Library, Victoria and Albert Museum (page 20); Mary Evans Picture Library, Swan Kettles (page 21); Nigel Luckhurst, John Riley/Consumer Association, Thomas Cook Ltd (page 22); John Riley (page 31); Crafts (page 32); Dick Powell, John Riley (page 34); John Riley (page 35); NASA/Science Photo Library (page 40); Crafts Council, Design Council, Earls Court and Olympia (page 42); Caroline Zianian (page 44); John Riley (page 45); John Riley/National Westminster Bank (page 46); Lloyd's of London (page 48); John Riley (page 50); Austin Rover Group Ltd (page 56); Paul Stead/Fitch and Co (page 57); Crafts (page 59); WWF (UK) Photo Library (page 60); BSI, Design Council (page 61); Paul Spooner (page 62); Crafts Council, House of Sweden (page 64); Seymour Powell (page 67); Paul Spooner (page 70); Crafts (page 72); Crafts, Crafts Council (page 73); Crafts Council/Alec McCurdy (page 74); Design Council/Rodney Kinsman, House of Sweden (page 76); John Riley, Science Photo Library (page 82); Science Photo Library (page 83); Paul Stead/Fitch and Co (page 84); John Riley (page 86); John Riley (page 87); NHPA (page 88); Associated Press Ltd, CharlesTait Photographic (page 90); Caroline Zianian (page 91); G Jones, Caroline Zianian (page 94); Caroline Zianian (page 95); G Jones (page 99); British Rail, British Steel Corporation, Central Electricity Generating Board, Science Photo Library (page 100).

We apologise to anybody that we have omitted from this list.

This book is designed to help pupils and teachers who are embarking on any of the new GCSE courses in Craft, Design and Technology, or CDT as we shall refer to it.

As you will know, there are three CDT courses for GCSE that your pupils can choose from which are outlined here:

CDT Design and Communication – which concentrates on the graphic communication of ideas for designing and making.

CDT Design and Realisation – which concentrates on three-dimensional product designing and making.

CDT Technology – which concentrates on the design and manufacture of technological products or systems.

The three courses represent slightly different approaches to what is essentially the same activity, that is designing and making things to solve problems and satisfy people's needs.

It is because of the close relationship between the three courses that we have chosen to describe the **common core** elements that will exist in all three courses at the start of this book. This common core covers the basic principles of designing, making and communicating that are vital for studying *any* of the three CDT courses. We have divided the common core into two parts.

**a** Being a designer – in which we introduce the activities that pupils will need to be familiar with in designing, making and evaluating.

**b** Being a consumer (or user) – in which we introduce ideas that pupils will need to think about as users of products in the present-day world and in the future. We believe that this section will be particularly useful for the CDT in Society elements of the courses.

Following the common core section, we look in more detail at each of the three CDT courses. These sections have been written by experienced teachers who have a huge number of ideas to contribute to developing the courses. Inevitably, the authors have brought their own style to the task, but their approach has been co-ordinated in four important respects.

**a** We have attempted to show how the courses build on the common core, but also allow for individual activity.

**b** All the sections have been designed as a series of double pages, each of which introduces new ideas and approaches.

**c** Each section introduces a wide range of project ideas within the context of the courses.

**d** Each section provides a GCSE examination checklist that will help you to use it and to see how the projects fit in with the overall balance and goals of the course.

CDT encompasses an enormously broad field of study, and it would be quite unrealistic to attempt to contain it all in a single short volume such as this one. Rather than this, what we have attempted to do is to provide ideas and starting points for project work, and to indicate the many ways in which they might be pursued and developed. We hope that this approach will help teachers in grappling with the evolution to GCSE and the increasingly pupil-centred requirements of teaching and learning.

### Your foundation course

In your first three years at secondary school did you ever design and make things like . . .

● an elastic band powered vehicle
● a greeting card
● a game or puzzle that needed building (or constructing)
● masks for a school production
● Working models such as Lego or Meccano
● a money or pencil box
● an ornamental light fitting
● some simple jewellery
● a mobile or another type of active toy?

If you did any of these sorts of projects, then you will be in a good position to use this book to help you to tackle the more advanced work that is required for GCSE. The 'foundation course' in CDT will have introduced you to the way you can go about tackling design problems, and you will be used to the idea that each project presents a number of problems which have to be solved and a number of decisions which have to be taken by you.

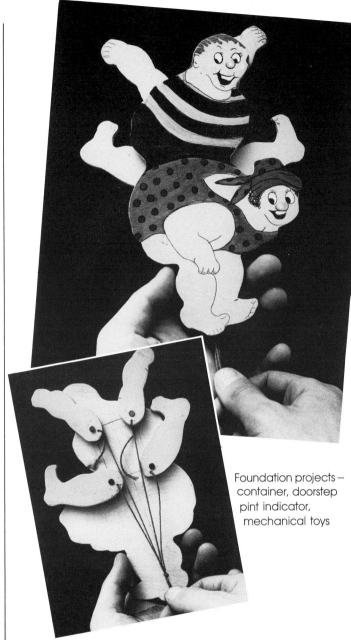

Foundation projects – container, doorstep pint indicator, mechanical toys

### Practical thinking

CDT projects usually result in you having to make things using materials and equipment, but there is a lot more to it than simply *making*. CDT projects start with finding the right problems to solve in the first place. It is only after you have done that that you have to decide whether you are taking sensible decisions to solve these problems. Some of your lessons might have involved you in using wood, metal, plastic, card, paper, ceramics or textiles, or in building simple electrical circuits or mechanical systems. If you did any of these things it would have been as part of a design project which involved you with practical problems and taking decisions. Were you asked to make simple models and draw out your ideas on paper? If so, you begin this course at an advantage. If not, do not worry, as this book will give you plenty of guidance.

## GCSE courses

GCSE courses in Craft, Design and Technology take you into considerably greater depth than is possible in the foundation course, and that is why it has been necessary to split the subject up into three courses. This enables you to choose which area of CDT you are most interested in studying further.

CDT Design and Communication concentrates on the graphic communication of ideas for designing and making.

CDT Design and Realisation concentrates on the three-dimensional product designing and making.

CDT Technology concentrates on the design and manufacture of technological products and systems.

This book will introduce you to all three courses, and you should talk to your teachers if you are not sure which one will suit you best.

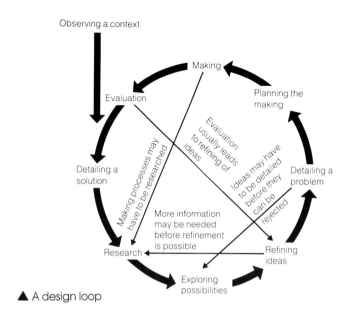

▲ A design loop

▼ Clockwork wriggler – a prototype for a set of power insect toys for children

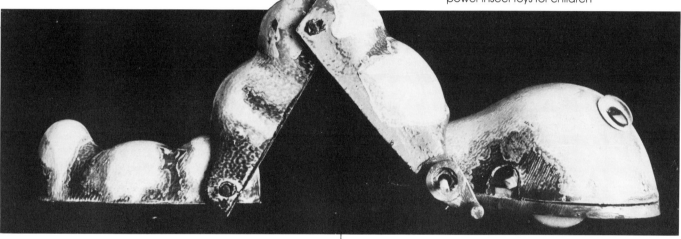

## Using this book

The first section of this book is common to all three of the course options. This 'common core' section is built around the **design loop** that you can use as a guide when doing any of your projects. Beyond that, some of the material becomes a little more specific to each of the options. However, you will find that even this more specialised material is helpful in each of the three options. For instance, if you are following a CDT Design and Communication course, you will use the first part of the book in common with people following the other two options.

However, you will also use the specialised Design and Communication section of the book in some detail. You will find that it is often helpful to dip into the other two specialised sections to get specific help on a particular topic.

You should use this book as a **guide** rather than as a source of all the information which you will require. In this book we only have space for the most basic ideas that will get you started on projects. You must go elsewhere for the more specialised information which you may require to carry your projects through to completion. Make sure that you make full use of your CDT teacher, who will be able to suggest ways of acquiring additional information, including other books, magazines and other specialist sources to be found inside and outside school. Knowing who to ask or where to look is a very important skill to develop.

Throughout this book you will find lots of questions, and lots of suggestions for activities and projects that you might do. You will find some in the actual text as you read it, and there are others which are set apart from the text in the 'activities' boxes, which appear on each double page spread. Attempt the short activities as you come across them, and talk to your teacher to see which of the longer projects might be the most suitable for you to tackle.

Finding problems to tackle is the starting point for all design activities. Design problems exist everywhere you look, for they are concerned with how *people live their lives* and how *products* and *systems* help them to do it. In any situation that you can imagine, think about *what* people are trying to do, *how* they are doing it, *what* systems or products they are making use of and *how* they might be improved. You will almost certainly find lots of design problems to tackle.

You spend a lot of time at home and at school, so these are good places to start when you want to look for design problems.

**Look at your school**

Here are three possible design problems that you might be asked to try to solve.

**a** Visitors are always coming to the school, but they can't find their way around and are constantly getting lost and having to ask for directions. How could you help them?
*(You could design a guide sheet, or a clear display model for the foyer.)*

**b** Too many of the teaching rooms are just doors off plain corridors, and visitors cannot distinguish between them.
*(You could design a corporate identity for different departments, so that the distinctive activities of that department were built into the structure and decor of its setting.)*

**c** The geography department has a small 'weather station' on the roof of the building. They would like a system so that all information gathered on the roof (rainfall, wind speed, temperature etc.) was constantly being displayed in the geography department.
*(You could design the system or a part of it.)*

**Look at your home**

Similarly, here are two problems that you may be asked to solve at home.

**a** Your backgarden bird-table is always being 'raided' by crows and starlings, so that the small, pretty birds are frightened away.
*(Design a bird-table that can only be used by the birds that you want to watch.)*

**b** Your mum would like a low light for the baby. She would ideally like it to have moving features that create interest.
*(Can you design the baby light – creating movement from the heat of the bulb?)*

As well as these two big areas of design opportunity, think about some of the other ways you spend your time, or the places that you are in. There will almost certainly be ways of improving them.

- Think about your leisure.
- Think about your transport.
- Think about how you carry things (by hand or on a bike).
- Think about how you leave messages.

When you are starting to solve a problem *always try to watch how other people do the same things*. You only have to open your eyes to see a design problem. But *seeing* the problem is only the first step. The next important activity is to get as much *information* as possible about the problem.

You need detailed information about the *people* involved, the *activity* they are involved in and the *situation* of the activity.

You have to ask yourself various questions about each element of the problem:

- **The people** – Who? How many? When? How often? How big? Why?

- **The activity** – What? When? How? How often? What's the difficulty? What's the cost? How long does it take?

- **The situation** – Where? Why? Where else? What environment? What cost? What's the difficulty?

Think about how you can best get hold of and record the information that you need. Is it by talking to people, by watching people, by listening, or by writing to people?

Collecting information under the three headings – people, activity and situation – should enable you to summarise your particular design problem clearly and in detail.

## Activities

1. Go in detail through 'a day in the life of' someone you know – or even yourself. Try to think through every 5 minutes, and you will soon find hundreds of things that were difficult, or awkward, or clumsy or badly organised. How to make them easier may well be the focus of a good design exercise.

2. For any of the design problems mentioned earlier (or one of your own) list the things you would have to find out about under the three headings – people, activity and situation.

3. For each of the three headings (people, activity and situation) list the ways that you could get hold of and record the information you need to try to solve your design problem.

Thinking for yourself is very important in CDT. It is something you need to do through all the stages of your project. It will help you to:

- identify a good project to tackle
- work out where to obtain information
- look for possible solutions to your problem
- decide on the details of your solution
- plan how best to communicate your ideas to others.

## So how do I get good ideas of my own?

Good ideas are very rarely completely new or original. They are usually existing ideas put together in different ways or applied to different situations. Try to remember the following sequence:

- **expand** your ideas by thinking up as many possibilities as you can
- **connect** your ideas by combining possibilities
- **contract** your thoughts by choosing the most promising idea or ideas.

Make sure you **record** all the ideas you have as your project progresses. If you forget an idea and you haven't recorded it you may have lost it for good.

## But what if I'm not a very 'creative' person?

Everybody, without exception, has the capacity to think imaginatively. It is a basic human ability that we all possess. But like many other abilities, if we don't practise it, it won't develop very much. Some techniques to practise are described below.

## OK, so where do I start?

The first thing to remember is that there is nothing worse than sitting staring at a blank sheet of paper waiting for ideas to suddenly 'happen'. Your mind will generally go as blank as the paper. You should begin by putting down whatever your first thoughts are – however basic or unlikely they might seem. Alternatively, you could start doodling and see what happens. No-one expects you to come up with a brilliant idea in your first sketch – and if you do they might be suspicious of where it came from!

## Try some of the following approaches

### 1 Brainstorming

Brainstorming is a very useful activity, in which you try to come up with as many ideas about a problem as you possibly can.

Let your mind wander freely around the problem. Put down as many ideas as you possibly can – but *don't judge them*. No-one is allowed to say whether an idea is silly or impossible or anything else. The point is to get ideas out of your head as fast as possible. Look for connections between things and ways in which usually unrelated things can be combined.

This activity can be done individually, but is *much more effective* in a group of up to six people. Someone must record all the ideas using words, sketches or both.

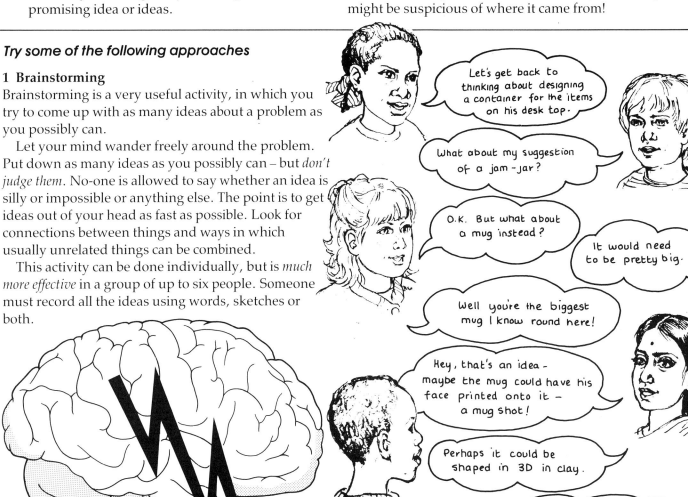

Let's get back to thinking about designing a container for the items on his desk top.

What about my suggestion of a jam-jar?

O.K. But what about a mug instead?

It would need to be pretty big.

Well you're the biggest mug I know round here!

Hey, that's an idea – maybe the mug could have his face printed onto it – a mug shot!

Perhaps it could be shaped in 3D in clay.

How could we make it easier to get the different items out?

▲ A short extract from a group brainstorming session – note how there is no criticism, and how ideas are built on previous suggestions.

## 2 Looking elsewhere

Ask yourself if there are any other completely different situations in which similar problems can be found. For instance, think about why British Rail commissioned a team of ship designers to work on a design for a train.

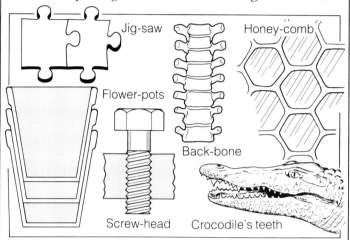

▲ Shapes that connect

## 3 Chance connections

Some of the best things seem to happen by chance. Try to encourage some 'happy accidents'.

- Go to the cupboard and take out the first thing you see.
- Open a dictionary at random. What is the first word you see?
- Turn on the TV. What is the first picture you see?
- Rearrange the letters of a keyword in your design brief. Can you make another word?

Whichever of these you try, see if you can establish a connection with your problem. You may uncover new possibilities.

• How many connections can you think of between a desk tidy and a train?
• How is the brain like a computer?
• Imagine you are a dice. Describe how you feel.

### When do I stop? How can I choose which ideas to develop?

You should stop only when there is no more time left. Then you must carefully **evaluate** your ideas. Some will be too costly, or too difficult to make or perhaps socially undesirable in other ways. Check back with the original specification and see which ideas best fit the problem. If there seems no way to choose between two good possibilities then toss a coin – take some risks and try to make the most of whatever happens. You can always come back to the idea that 'lost' if you want to.

Having your own ideas is not easy. It often takes courage to begin with, but in the end you can stand back and see that your project is different from other people's – in some way it is individual and yours.

Believe in your own ideas, even if they need a lot of developing before they can be used successfully. Always remember that having good ideas involves:

- trying things out
- not worrying if things aren't always right first time
- letting go of being a perfectionist
- making the most of whatever happens
- being patient
- long hours of struggle
- a real sense of achievement.

## Activities

1. Brainstorm the following problems:
   - improving school uniforms
   - road safety
   - getting to school on time.
   
   What other topics could you suggest to brainstorm?

2. On your own, sketch thirty possibilities for:
   - measuring intervals of time
   - things which move on wheels
   - uses of devices for sitting on
   - applications for artificial light sources.

3. Make a collection of visual images (sketches, pictures etc.) and verbal statements (phrases, jokes, poems, song titles and so on) based on the following themes:
   - space travel
   - cityscape
   - black and white
   - jumpers.
   
   Present a collage of each on an A3 sheet of paper.

▲ Collage sheet on the theme of breakfast time

However good your design ideas are they will be worthless if you cannot **communicate** them effectively to other people. It is also important to be able to understand and interpret information that other people communicate to you. Good communication will help you to:

- retrieve and record important information about your design problem
- discuss ideas as they develop
- convey the details of your solution to whoever will be involved in making or carrying out your ideas
- convince your teacher and the examiner of the quality and quantity of your ideas.

### *How can you improve your communication skills?*

The best way to start is by being aware of the numerous ways in which we all send and receive information every day. The messages that are sent are usually about:

- how things are (like a particular day's menu)
- how things were (like an old building)
- how things might be (like a proposed design)
- how we think and feel about what is happening (like in a diary).

In all of the types of message mentioned above the impact of **visual** communication is very important. A picture can tell a thousand words, but drawings by themselves are unlikely to be completely sufficient to convey your ideas.

Really effective communication usually involves a rich mixture of words, pictures and numbers – and often even physical gestures and actions.

▲ The past          ▲ The present

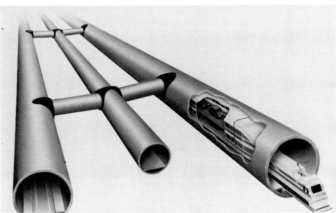

▲ The future

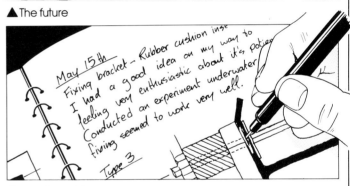

▲ Your thoughts

**Words** both written and spoken are probably the most commonly used form of communication. They are also important to our thinking. When the mind is thinking it is talking to itself.

**Visual images** or pictures dominate our lives far more than we realise – through signs, trademarks, drawings, photographs, film and television. Surprisingly though, people are generally much less fluent in using these forms of communication than they are with words. When attempting to make visual statements, their permanance and impact can often be intimidating. It is easier to fudge issues with words – but designers can't afford to fudge things. Designers must develop the confidence to make their visual statements clear to others.

**Numbers** are particularly efficient for communicating details of **quantity** – such things as time, cost, weight, size, strength and location.

But you should also remember the importance of **body language** in people's lives. How they look, their hair styles, their clothes and how they sit, stand, move and communicate with others. These things all say a lot about a person and how they want to be identified.

### How do you decide which method to use to communicate your design proposal?

Remember that you will probably need to use a mixture of approaches, and before you can decide the best ways, you need to think about the following questions:

SENDER

- ● WHAT information and ideas do I have to communicate?
- ● WHY am I sending these messages – what do I hope to achieve?
- ● WHEN shall I be sending the message – time, place and circumstance?
- ● HOW MUCH detail is needed?
- ● WHO am I communicating to?

The last of these questions is *very important*. It is a good rule to remember to try to imagine that you are receiving the message instead of sending it – and then consider the questions opposite.

RECEIVER

- ● HOW MUCH do I already know about the situation?
- ● AM I going to find the information INTERESTING?
- ● HOW IMPORTANT is it for me to understand or remember the information?
- ● HOW am I likely to react? Will I be pleased, annoyed, surprised?
- ● HOW am I going to communicate my response back to someone?

Whichever of the three CDT courses you are doing, you will find the 'Checklist' of graphic communication techniques on pages 52 and 53 particularly useful at this point.

## Activities

1. Your family are hoping to arrange to exchange their house with a family in America for a month next summer. A very brief description of your house has already been published in a hand-book, and you have now received several enquiries from interested families asking for further details.

   Design and produce the art work for a double-sided A4 sheet which could be photocopied and sent to the families. It will need to provide the necessary factual information, and make your house seem as attractive as possible.

2. The local council have just announced plans for routing a new road (or a pedestrianisation scheme) in your neighbourhood. Assume that you disagree with their intentions and have a better idea. Consider and present ways in which you could make your views known to the council in such a way that they are likely to take notice of them.

# Modelling Ideas

As you start to develop your initial ideas in more detail you will need to:

- discuss your ideas with other people
- evaluate and modify your ideas
- explore further possibilities when difficulties arise.

To help you achieve these things more effectively, you can represent your ideas by means of a series of two- and three-dimensional models.

## What are models in the design context?

Models are simplified versions of the intended real thing. Because they are simpler, they are also easier, quicker and cheaper to make, but can still allow you to explore your ideas in detail.

A pupil was developing ideas for an adjustable chair, and used a series of simple, small-scale card models in order to:

- see what the idea would look like in 3D
- discuss with staff how to proceed
- explore ways of changing the proportions of the various components
- suggest completely new possibilities
- test the principle of adjustment.

## How simple should a model be?

The simpler the model, the easier it will be to create, but the less informative it will be in predicting how the design will finally work. One of the things the card models of the chair could not reveal was whether or not the structure was comfortable – a very important consideration.

Don't forget that words, sketches, drawings and numbers are all types of model as well, because they serve to represent reality in a simplified way.

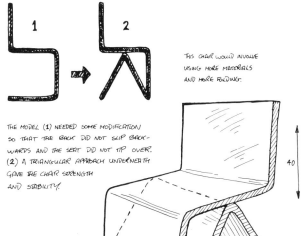

1   2

THIS CHAIR WOULD INVOLVE USING MORE MATERIALS AND MORE FOLDING.

THE MODEL (1) NEEDED SOME MODIFICATION SO THAT THE BACK DID NOT SLIP BACK-WARDS AND THE SEAT DID NOT TIP OVER. (2) A TRIANGULAR APPROACH UNDERNEATH GAVE THE CHAIR STRENGTH AND STABILITY.

## So what sort of model should you choose?

To get the right information from models often means that you must use several different types of model to test different sorts of ideas. What you need to do is to choose the right types of model to test the particular ideas that you are interested in. Think carefully about the information you need from your model. What aspects of the idea do you want to explore? You might consider using a model that:

- changes the **scale** of the idea by making the model smaller (or larger) than the final design will be
- changes the **material** by using something easier or cheaper to work with
- changes the **form** of the idea by exploring a three-dimensional (3D) idea in a two-dimensional (2D) model.

Often, models will have to use a combination of change of scale, material and form.

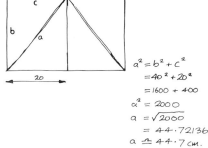

$$a^2 = b^2 + c^2$$
$$= 40^2 + 20^2$$
$$= 1600 + 400$$
$$a^2 = 2000$$
$$a = \sqrt{2000}$$
$$= 44.72136$$
$$a \doteq 44.7 \text{ cm}.$$

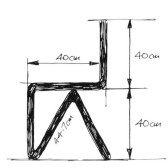

## Mental modelling

Don't forget that the most sophisticated modelling tool you have is your own brain. In your 'mind's eye' you can create and change complex design ideas that combine 2D and 3D images, words and numbers. You can also do it at speeds and levels of sophistication as yet unmatched by most computer systems.

Unfortunately, this mental modelling is very private, and if you are to share your ideas and explore them with other people you will still need to make 'real' models to explain your thinking. You will also find that getting your thoughts out of your head and onto paper and into modelling materials will help you to sharpen and clarify the ideas.

> *An exact model is designed to convey an idea as faithfully as possible. One that works, such as the 'Slimbeam' torch, completes the illusion of realism and enables the user to assess its performance fully. In CDT, the combination of working circuitry and packaging provides a challenge greater than the sum of the two problems taken separately.*
>
> John Cave

From the Thames TV series
*Craft, Design and Technology*

In the problem shown above, a pupil wanted to check the heights and positions of doors, shelves and control units for a wardrobe for handicapped children.

He modelled his ideas by making a full size (but 2D) representation by using coloured tape. It was quick and easy to transport to the location where the real wardrobe was to be used.

The project illustrated here concerned the design of a tractor seat suspension system. A quickly

adjustable framework model was made and fitted to the tractor cab so that different angles and positions of the seat could be explored and evaluated.

In this example, small-scale 3D models of kitchen units were made in card to enable a pupil to explore different room layouts.

## Activities

1. For each illustration of a model on this page, state whether the designer has changed the form, scale, and/or material of the final object. Mention a number of important aspects of the designs which could *not* have been modelled adequately in each case.

2. For each of the things listed below, think of three different appropriate models a designer could use. Explain your thoughts in full, describing the uses, advantages and disadvantages of each model.
   - i) A motor car
   - ii) A house
   - iii) A mechanical toy
   - iv) A television commercial

3. A flow chart is a graphic model. Choose one of the following activities and analyse the sequence of events in the order in which they occur. Think about the elements of the activity you need to model. Draw up a flow chart and ask someone else to follow it. Record what happens and modify your design as necessary.
   - i) Making breakfast
   - ii) Getting up in the morning
   - iii) Replacing a fuse
   - iv) Mending a puncture

# Prototyping – Making What You Have Designed

Suppose that you have generated and developed an idea in response to a design brief, and have reached the stage at which you want to make the product. This is called the **realisation** stage, and it often takes up the majority of the time available to the whole project. It is very important to get it right.

## So where do you start?

Your design idea will need to be worked out in such a way that the detail required for the realisation is clearly communicated in a **working drawing**. This must contain constructional details, sizes, materials and finishes, as well as a cutting list or parts list.

The realisation itself can be divided into two stages.
**a** Preparation
**b** Manufacture

## Preparation
### (i) Planning

Working with your CDT teacher, you should **plan** your approach to the manufacturing stage. You should work out a procedure to be followed and, ideally, an indication of the amount of time available for each part of that procedure. If you attempt to keep to your schedule you are much less likely to 'drift' and more likely to make full use of the time available. You will soon find that time is extremely precious – you never have as much of it as you would like. Keep to your schedule as closely as you can, and remember that if you slip a bit one week you will have to make it up somewhere else.

You may find it helpful to keep a running 'slip chart' to remind you of what stage you should be at at a particular time, and how much you have slipped from your original schedule.

### (ii) Practising

Another important aspect of the preparation is the practising of any techniques with which you are

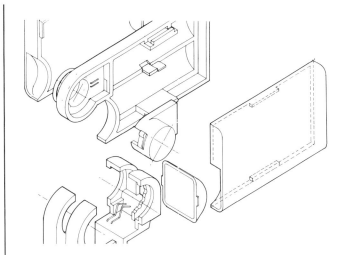

▲ Part of a working diagram of a Durabeam torch

unfamiliar. Sometimes you are confident of developing your skills as you go along, but it is nearly always wise to practise first, especially if there is a lot at stake. Check this detail with your CDT teacher.

### (iii) Getting hold of materials

You will need to select and collect together the materials which you require. Certain materials may be available from a stock in school, but other materials, such as dry letter press, special electronic components or precious metals, may have to be purchased locally or by mail order. Some of this you may have to undertake for yourself.

Whatever materials you get, check them carefully against your specification. Wherever possible choose materials of good quality, as these are likely to be the easiest to use and give the best possible finish to a realisation. However, you must always remember that cost is of great importance, and if you spend too much on materials, you will have to cut back somewhere else.

| Name _____ | Form _____ | Project _____ | | |
|---|---|---|---|---|
| Week | Work scheduled | Slip | Work completed | Teacher's signature |
| 1<br>Date | | | | |
| 2<br>Date | | | | |
| 3<br>Date | | | | |
| 4<br>Date | | | | |

## Stages of manufacture

The actual processes of manufacture will differ according to the type of project you are working on. Some of the more specific detail may be found elsewhere in this book or from other sources. There are some general points for you to keep in mind. You should work **carefully** and **methodically**, attempting to think ahead so that the consequences of your current actions will not create problems later in your design process.

You should work **precisely**, checking each stage carefully and frequently. There is a saying, 'Think three times, check twice and cut once'.

Use your **design folio** as a reference during the realisation stage. It is surprisingly easy to become carried away in the manufacture of something, and the eventual outcome is very different from the intended one. Certain details are almost inevitably altered during manufacture and you need to keep a record of them.

It is often the case that unforeseen problems arise during realisation. These affect the intended outcome of the project and should be taken into consideration at the next stage – **evaluation**. It is quite usual, and perfectly proper, for modifications to be developed during realisation. This is why we talk of a design *process*.

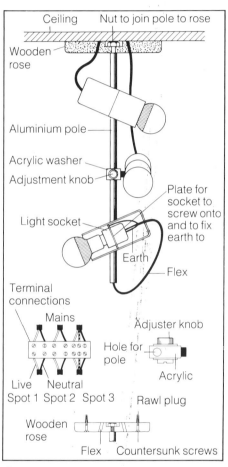

▲ Detail it before you draw it

## What about things which cannot be made?

Sometimes a 'final' realisation is not appropriate to a particular CDT project. If a new layout for a shopping precinct is being projected, there is little possibility of realising that idea in any other form than a model. There is a difference, however, between this sort of model-making and the 'modelling' of ideas that we referred to on pages 14 and 15. Making a model may well be appropriate as a realisation of a particular design, for instance, if the design is too large or too complex to make 'for real'. Modelling, on the other hand, is an activity carried out at a previous stage in your designing, when you are working out your ideas.

## Activities

1. Think of a number of realisations of a non-permanent nature, for example, a design for stage make-up, a hair style or a shop window arrangement. How might a record best be kept of these? Remember that it might be necessary to **assess** the realisation at a later date.

2. Above are some photographs of some realised designs. Can you work out the ways in which they were made and draw up the procedure which was worked through?

3. From the drawing can you work out and present the material requirements for the realisation? If the wooden ceiling component broke during manufacture what would the various options be to complete the realisation?

# Evaluation – Weighing Up the Pros and Cons

Once your design has been realised you should be prepared to make your own **evaluation** of your project. You must treat it as an initial prototype, or provisional solution, and attempt to describe the alterations you would make if you were given the opportunity to make a second model or begin a production run.

### What should you evaluate?

There are four areas which need to be analysed in order to produce an evaluation of your project:

  i)   performance against the original brief
  ii)  appearance and aesthetics
  iii) the accuracy of the realisation against the initial design
  iv)  personal feelings.

For the first two of these you are evaluating the **outcome** or **product** of your designing. The second two are evaluating your designing as a **process** that you actually worked through.

The obvious starting point in evaluating is to check the performance of the realised idea against the original **specification** or **design brief**. This is an evaluation of **function**.

The **appearance** of the realised idea is an important consideration, and an **evaluation** of it is vital. What aspects of appearance do you think it is important for you to evaluate? Why is the evaluation of appearance more difficult than the evaluation of function?

In any project it is often necessary to make some **compromises** as you work through it. Perhaps you did not have enough time, or you had to use cheaper but inferior quality of material. Whether this had a bad effect on the result, or whether you found ways of overcoming the problems is an evaluation of the **resourcing** of the project.

Finally, you can make a **personal** evaluation of the project. What thoughts do you have about the level of satisfaction you got from working on the project? Do you feel that it has been a success or a failure for you? You are also best placed to decide whether or not you have tried as hard as you could have done and worked carefully enough to achieve the best possible results.

### Making evaluations needs information

You will need to think about the best form of collecting information for your evaluation. This might be a test, a questionnaire, a book, a tape recording or photographs, or a combination of all of these. A good source of information is the project diary which you ought to keep. Your evaluation may take the form of a written report or it might form a part of a display, and therefore use a more visual approach, with drawings, photographs and charted results.

Whatever the form of the presentation, it should include all the information you have been able to collect and the conclusions you are able to draw from it.

EVALUATION

1. HOW WELL DOES THE PRODUCT DO ITS JOB?
I have not had much chance but I did present the toy to a child of four years old along with several other shop bought toys. The child played about with all of the toys one after another and after about 10 minutes the child picked up two pieces hit them together a few times and then to my delight put them together. The child picked up another part, lost interest, dropped them and left the room.

2. HAVE ANY ALTERATIONS BEEN MADE TO THE ORIGINAL DESIGN DURING MANUFACTURE? WHY?
The only change was that I did not construct as many accessories as I was going to as they were proving to be more time consuming than I had expected.

3. COULD YOU HAVE MADE IT BETTER?
The only problems that I found on the craftsmanship was that the wood sealer was difficult to apply in the grooves of the blocks and this does look untidy.

Shower unit for the disabled

❝ The question of pupils evaluating their own work is very important now within GCSE because it raises the issues, not only of 'does my product or system work?', but, in a wider sense, 'having gone through this process, was it a sensible problem to tackle?'. ❞

Richard Kimbell

Make sure that you distinguish between facts – **objective** and **testable** statements – and opinions – **subjective** personal judgements. Your tests should be as objective as possible, and any subjective statements which you use need to be carefully justified if they are to have any meaning. Like any designer, if you are to improve, you have to be prepared for your work to be criticised.

**A checklist of evaluation questions**

1. Have you tested your realisation in its intended setting?
2. Does your realised idea work in the way that was intended?
3. Have any difficulties with the operation been noted?
4. How could you improve the function?
5. Is your realisation well produced?
6. How could the standard of manufacture be improved?
7. Have you used the best materials and construction for the object?
8. State the best features of your realisation, such as finish, accuracy of construction etc.
9. Is it possible to compare your project with a commercially-produced item? Comment on any improvements or changes which you feel you could make or have made already.
10. List the comments which other people have made about your work. Who did you ask to comment and why? Whose opinions do you think you need to take notice of to improve your design?
11. Does the realisation match the idea presented in your design folio?
12. State the reasons for any differences which have occurred.
13. Where did the idea for your design come from?
14. State the best features of your idea, such as novelty value, simplicity etc.
15. Have you made a good job of presenting your design folio?
16. Did you complete the realisation in the time available? If not, why not?
17. With what did you need most help and where did the help come from?
18. Which aspects of the project did you most enjoy?

## Activities

1. Using the questions above, or others of your own, evaluate a project which you have worked on and write a report that covers all the appropriate points.

2. Study the two items in the photographs above. One is a screw-top bottle opener made out of metal and acrylic sheet, the other is an idea for a shop sign. Write out the procedure you would adopt to conduct a thorough evaluation of them. What additional information do you need about them to complete a design?

3. Write down a list of the type of questions you would ask if you wanted to gauge public opinion of a proposal for an adventure playground. Imagine that you are a parent of a potential user of the playground or a person who lives next door to the site. Does this affect the questions or the people you would ask?

4. Describe the ways in which you would evaluate the chess game and the record sleeve shown here.

History is not just about remembering where and when great battles took place, or who were the kings and queens of England. It's about seeing how people have dealt with the circumstances they were in – and how we can learn from their experiences. So is it too with CDT. We look into history to see the consequences that have followed from the development of new products and systems. We look to see how the lives of designers, manufacturers and, most importantly, users have been transformed by the growth of our industrialised society.

### Why are things the way they are?

By looking at the development of designed products, we are more able to think about why they became the way they did. By taking a specific topic we can see how the complex mixture of technological, economic, social, cultural and even political factors have influenced its development. The spindly legs of classic 18th Century furniture (that of Chippendale, Hepplewhite and friends) would not have been technically sound in English hardwoods like oak and walnut. These timbers were suitable for the heavy furniture typical of the 17th Century, but not for the later delicate products. The first importation of mahogany from Honduras, in the new colonies, towards the end of the 17th Century brought about dramatic changes in traditional furniture design.

Similarly, the extremely expensive, lockable, silver tea-caddies of the 18th Century suggest that

in those days tea was a precious and highly prized commodity. Trade, economics, politics, design and technology have always co-existed and affected each other.

> 6 A useful way of understanding why the objects which surround us look the way they do is to study their past. By looking at the way they have evolved over the years – at the technical, social and cultural reasons why they have changed – it is possible to see today's objects as part of a continuous process, and to understand them much more clearly as a result. 9

Penny Sparke

THAMES

### Finding out about the history of products and systems

Your first task is to choose an area that interests you. Are you interested in technological systems – like signal systems for communication or computing? Are you interested in transport systems? (When were the first traffic lights introduced? Where? Why? Who paid for them? What happened before?) Or are you interested in the development of domestic or industrial products? (When were the first plastic billiard balls made? What did they use before? Who made the first cigarette?)

Your local library will be a rich source for books or newspapers of the period you choose to study. You might be able to talk to the people who lived then (if it wasn't too long ago) and study the products first hand in museums. Look for connections with other people and events and see if you can trace the evolution of the product or system. Don't forget to keep a thorough record of all your research.

## Activities

Make a detailed study of an aspect of the development of one of the following:
- electricity in the home
- concrete in buildings
- railways
- bicycles
- the high street
- the microchip
- telecommunications
- food packaging.

Throughout each day you are constantly making choices and taking decisions about the way you spend your life. You consider the things you are going to do, the places you are going to visit and the goods and servies you are likely to need.

In today's advanced industrial society there is a huge range of goods and services to choose from. Choosing wisely, and getting value for money involves spending time and effort. Never buy the first thing you see without evaluating it. There are often a whole range of brands to select from, and then different models available at different prices.

### So how do you choose?

The best approach is to apply the skills of researching and evaluating which were discussed on pages 8, 9, 18 and 19. It is important to start by asking the right questions about:
● what you need  ● what you want  ● where it can be obtained  ● when it is required  ● how much you should pay  ● whether it will last for the time you need it for  ● whether it can be mended easily and cheaply  ● where or from whom information about it can be obtained.

This last point is particularly important. There are lots of magazines now that specialise in providing information on consumer matters. The *Which?* magazine is probably the most well known. But don't forget that there are many sources of information:
   ● shop assistants
   ● sales brochures and literature
   ● independent reports (like *Which?*)
   ● friends and relatives
   ● your own tests or trials.
Remember that it may be wise to use more than one source of information to get a balanced impression of a subject.

Consider how you could adapt the checklist on page 19 to make it suitable for evaluating something which you might want to buy. Don't forget to consider all aspects of the product – not just its technical performance. What is it about it that appeals to you visually or emotionally? Will it make you feel happier, more secure, more important or more individual?

### Choosing for someone else

So far we have considered how to set about choosing things for ourselves. Quite often in life you have to make decisions about the things other people need and want. The questions which you have to ask when choosing for someone else are similar to those you would ask yourself. Remember that a very useful design skill is to be able to place yourself in the shoes of another person and attempt to project how they are likely to think and feel.

To see how different people's reactions might be to any product just think about the sorts of questions that designers, manufacturers, financial investors, users and advertisers might ask. They will all see goods and services from completely different viewpoints.

## It all depends on your point of view

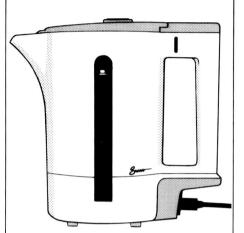

### THE MANUFACTURER

- Did manufacturing this kettle exploit my particular knowledge and expertise in plastics and moulding techniques?
- Was I able to sell it at a price which covered my production costs and made a profit for the shareholders?
- Did it enhance my reputation in the marketplace so that people will buy our other products on the strength of our name?

### THE MARKETING DIRECTOR

- How well did we manage to predict what sort of kettle people would need and want, and how much they would be prepared to pay for it?
- Did the way it was promoted effectively inform the public of its qualities and its potential value to them?
- Is everybody happy and satisfied?

### THE DESIGNER

- Will it appeal to potential customers?
- Does it follow current stylistic trends?
- Have the various components been designed to be cost-effective in production?
- Will the client like it?
- Will it win a design award?

### THE FAMILY

- Does it match the rest of our kitchen?
- Is it easy to operate?
- Is it available now?
- Is it reliable?
- Will our neighbours admire it?

### THE ELDERLY RELATIVE

- Is it more than I can afford?
- Can I pour from it easily?
- Is there any danger of scalding myself from the steam?
- What happens if I forget to switch it off?
- Is it as solid and well made as my old kettle?
- Will it help me to retain my independence?

## Activities

1. The illustration above shows some of the questions different people might ask about the design of an electric kettle. What other questions does each person need to consider?

2. Choose a particular model of one of the following and evaluate it from the points of view of the user, the designer and the manufacturer:
   - a vacuum cleaner
   - a domestic cooker
   - a personal stereo
   - a clock radio
   - a magazine or newspaper
   - a local shopping centre
   - your local transport system.
   
   Establish its position in the market, and compare it with other similar competitive products.

3. Using the points given above make a detailed analysis of a product or service you have recently purchased. How well does it meet your needs? Present your analysis visually.

4. Try making separate lists of the goods and services which you require for a day at school. Be careful to recognise the differences between things you *need* and the things that you *want*.

# Success or Failure – In the Balance

Through design we try to improve the conditions in which we live our lives. But for every improvement there seems to be a cost – and sometimes people wonder if the balance is right. As well as giving some improvement, most products do some damage to us or our world in one way or another, and in the end we must be responsible for striking the right balance.

❝ *Nothing we design or make ever really works. We can always say what it ought to do, but that it never does. The aircraft falls out of the sky or rams the earth at full tilt and kills people. It has to be tended like a new-borne babe. It drinks like a fish. Its life is measured in hours. Our dinner table ought to be variable in size and height, removeable altogether, impervious to scratches, self-cleaning, and having no legs. The motor car ought to stop dead, and no one in it be thrown forward, in the same instant that you press a button. We cannot console ourselves with the belief that such things are impossible. Who would ever have believed that a child could light a whole room by moving its finger?* ❞

(From Pye, D. (1964) The Nature of Design, Studio Vista.)

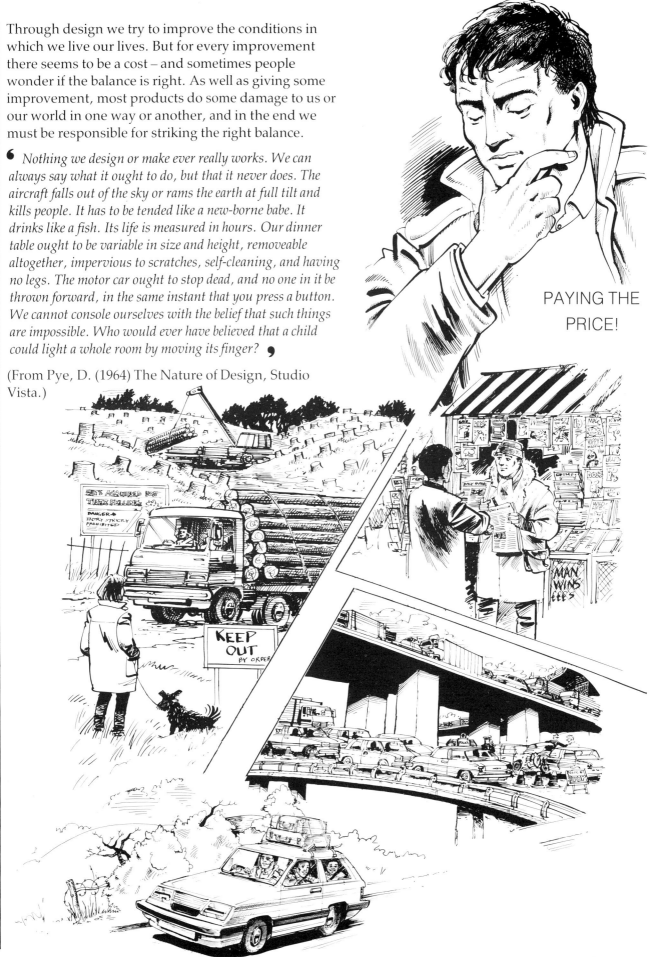

PAYING THE PRICE!

## Values for life

Consider the ways in which design, technology and the associated commerce have served us by:

BENEFITS . . . . .

- making our domestic and working lives easier, safer, healthier and longer
- enabling us to travel much greater distances and much faster
- allowing us to communicate with each other far more effectively, more quickly and over greater distances
- creating greater wealth and prosperity for more people
- providing us with a wide range of goods and services to choose from in order to satisfy our needs and wants

PENALTIES . . . . .

- concentrating our population into huge impersonal conurbations and creating a high stress environment with many social problems
- generating waste matter, some of it very dangerous, faster than we can deal with it
- causing injury and suffering through industrial accidents and disasters
- using and not replenishing many of the earth's natural resources
- wiping out many past traditions, rituals and cultures
- persuading people to desire things which they do not really need or want

Is technological change for the better or worse?

There is never a simple 'yes' or 'no' answer to this question. All developments in design, technology and commerce bring benefits and penalties. What is important is the point of balance between the two. The equilibrium is decided by what is felt to be acceptable to society as a whole – and that means **you** should have an opinion about it.

We each need to think about, decide and take action to try and bring about the sort of world we want to live in. All too often we sit back and let others influence and manipulate our surroundings and circumstances. Although we often complain to each other, we rarely try to do much about things which we think may be wrong.

## Activities

1. Assume that you have been asked to design the following products. List the benefits and the penalties to you (the designer), the manufacturer, the user and the general public.
   - an advertisement for cigarettes
   - a new energy-efficient car that seems likely to halve the fuel consumption, but to have only half the performance of a conventional car
   - a fashion garment made from real animal skin
   - a fashion garment made from a synthetic plastic
   - a telephone bugging system

2. Select a current technological issue which interests you. Prepare a presentation – or write an illustrated magazine article – which gives a completely balanced view (benefits and penalties) of the situation.

# Preparing for the Future

The future is closer than you think. It is relatively easy to predict the very near future, but the further away in time the more difficult it gets to predict what will happen. Here are some questions to give you some idea of how difficult it can be to predict what will happen.

- What do you think you will be doing in five years' time?
- Where will you be living?
- What will you be wearing?
- What things will be very important to you?
- What do you want your life to be like?

It might surprise you to know that designers and manufacturers are already taking decisions about things which will influence your life well into the future, such as the design of cars which will appear in five years' time, the planning of road networks, new towns, financial investment services and so on. Many of these things take a very long time to design and develop, so it is important to think well ahead. How long will it be before the Channel Tunnel is completed and in operation? And what sort of effects is that going to have on people?

▲ Still from 'Metropolis'

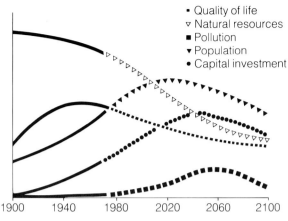

- ▪ Quality of life
- ▽ Natural resources
- ▪ Pollution
- ▼ Population
- ● Capital investment

▲ MIT global trends

The demand for particular services and products can be approximately predicted into the next century by using current information on the size of the population. These statistical predictions are very unreliable, however, as trends in demand tend to change with time. See if you can find out about what the projected use of the Humber road bridge or the M25 London orbital motorway was at the time they were first designed. How accurate were the predictions, and can you explain any big inaccuracies?

### How can you set about designing for the future?

The best approach is to try to make some of your own forecasts based not only on what is statistically *likely* to happen but also on what you feel *ought* to happen.

By combining your thoughts and dreams of how you would like to live with *realistic* projections of technological developments, it is possible to create some visions of what the nature and quality of your life might be like in the future.

Such visions can prove to be extremely valuable, not so much as accurate predictions, but more for the influence they can have on you and other people when decisions are taken about the shape of the future.

## Activities

1. Choose one of the topics presented on the next page, and consider the questions posed underneath. Present your responses in a clear and lively manner in order to attract attention, stimulate interest and make other people think about the possible changes in the nature and quality of their lives in the future.

2. Imagine it is the 21st Century, and plans are being made to set up a small space station on the Moon. Do some research to discover the sorts of structure in which it might be possible to live and work, and what technological advances still need to be achieved.

3. How would you feel if you were invited to be one of the first group of people to live and work on the Moon? Make a list of the things you would be most glad to get away from, and another of the things you would really miss. Which of your personal belongings would you take with you? What sorts of advantages might there be, and what would be the major disadvantages?

26

SOME STARTING POINTS FOR THINKING ABOUT HOW THE FUTURE MIGHT BE — WHAT OTHERS CAN YOU IDENTIFY?

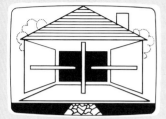

**THE HOME**
The living room / The kitchen
The Workshop / The garage
Furniture / Domestic appliances

**THE HIGH STREET**
Shop interiors. Pedestrian
walkways. Shopping Malls
Street signs and Furniture

**TRANSPORT**
Bicycles, Cars, Trains
Aeroplanes, Space-flight

**COMMUNICATIONS**
Television / Interactive video
Optical fibres / Miniaturisation

**ENERGY**
Nuclear fuel, Solar energy
Wave and Wind power

**CLOTHING**
Materials, Function, Styles
Accessories

**LEISURE**
Sport. Entertainment
Recreation

**SECURITY**
In the home. On the streets
Vandalism

**THE COUNTRYSIDE**
Animals, Plants
Rights of way

**FOOD**
Preparation, Chemical additives
Diet, Presentation

**HEALTH**
Medicines, Hospitals
Bio-engineering

**EDUCATION**
Schools, Colleges
Distance Learning

What is the present situation like?

How might things change for the better

.... or for the worse?

What would I like to see happening?

How is it likely to change over the next 5, 10, 20 years?

What technological and social advances would be necessary?

Why is this important? Why am I concerned?

What other aspects of life might change as a result?

In what ways does it concern other people?

What can I do to help bring about the changes I would like to see?

So far this book has been concerned with the aspects of CDT which are common to all the three course options. On these two pages we will try to show you how any everyday situation might be used as the starting point for design projects that could fit into the three specialist CDT options.

Remember that the three options are:
● CDT Design and Communication
● CDT Design and Realisation
● CDT Technology.

It is also important to remember that these courses are different in **emphasis** only. The first emphasises the communication aspects of design, whilst the last emphasises the technological aspects. But all three are concerned with designing, making and communicating, so it would be quite possible for very similar projects to fit into all three of the courses.

Look at the illustration below. It is a very ordinary scene in an infant school, with a group of young children working in a corner of their classroom. Whichever of the three CDT courses you are studying, if you went to look carefully at a scene like this you should be able to identify a range of problems that you could tackle. One group of pupils noted the following potential design problems, which have been listed by the course option that the problem most obviously fits into.

## CDT Design and Realisation

The sand tray was always spilling sand all over the floor.

There was an untidy heap of papers, books and craft materials on the teacher's desk.

When the young children did paintings, they had to leave them laid out on tables overnight to dry.

The reading scheme that was used by the teacher needed separate sets of books kept in a number of closed trays. The children had to keep asking the teacher which tray to look in because the system was confusing.

The children really wanted a special bird table outside the window to attract particular types of birds.

The children wanted to develop a simple plant-propagating area in the corner window of the classroom.

The teacher used a system of shoe boxes for storing art and craft materials. They kept getting mixed up and damaged by the constant use.

## CDT Technology

The weather and temperature chart that the pupils filled in every day was very unreliable. They wanted a system that constantly recorded the changing conditions.

The children kept a lot of plants in the classroom, but they still needed to be watered at weekends and in the holidays.

The goldfish and gerbils also needed feeding over weekends and half terms.

The children were learning to tell the time, and the teacher thought that a simple game (perhaps using lights and buzzers) might excite them and help them to learn more quickly.

Mechanical toys with parts that move in unexpected and interesting ways are always fun to play with. Especially if the mechanisms can be seen and modified by the children.

If the pupils get their plant propagator built in the corner window, it would be good if it could have a control system built into it to adjust the temperature and moisture level.

## CDT Design and Communication

It is hard for the children to find the right places to put books and games back on the shelves and in the cupboards.

There was a large wall chart used to record the changing weather and seasons. But it was dull and rather uninteresting.

The blinds were very drab and rather worn.

The fire-drill notice was typed onto a piece of ordinary paper. It was difficult to read and certainly not very eye-catching.

There was a large blank brick wall just outside the classroom.

The teacher was hoping to acquire a new 'play-shop' for the corner of the room, but the school couldn't afford it.

Some of the children were rehearsing a play for glove puppets. They had written the play but were still hoping to make the puppets and scenery.

## Activities

1. Think about some of the problems listed above. Many of them are not yet detailed into design problems that could be tackled. Pick one or two that interest you and detail them with all the information you think would be needed to get started on designing a solution.

2. We have suggested here the likely course that the problems might fit into. Can you see how some of the problems could be detailed in such a way that the emphasis of the project changed and made it more suitable for a different CDT option?

Look carefully at the drawing above. Under the headings of 'The Home', 'The Environment', 'Industry' and 'Education' make a list of all the examples of how information and ideas are being communicated visually.

Recent technological developments have helped to make the processes of communication more efficient, quicker, easier and cheaper. Knowing **how** to use technology as an aid to communication has become an essential everyday skill. Even more important, however, is knowing **which** methods to use and **when** to use them.

The following pages in this section present a series of opituations and activities which can be used as starting points for the identification of problems of **design and communication**. A series of activities is presented that will be suitable for your course project

work. You don't have to stick rigidly to the briefs suggested, but discuss any changes with your teacher.

You might also like to look at pages 52–55, where you will see a comprehensive guide to the skills and techniques that you will use on a design and communication course. It will help you see where your present project fits in the overall course.

Finally, look carefully at the way in which the graphic presentation of each double page has been designed. Drawings, photographs and text have been related in a variety of ways involving cut-outs, shadows, overlaps, changes of scale, speech bubbles, tones etc. They are intended to give each page more visual impact. Do you think it works? Could you use similar ideas when you plan and present your own work?

## Fun and games

This first theme is concerned with projects involving the design of toys, games and play spaces for children. Through such activities you can provide opportunities to:

- develop skills
- pretend you are someone else (a detective or a famous explorer)
- take risks (knowing that there is no real danger)
- be competitive
- be part of a team.

Some games are highly organised, with complicated rules and playing pieces. Others are little more than a simple play space that will stimulate children's own ideas for games.

## Learning through play

Playing and learning go hand in hand. Toys and games involve children in developing important skills in communication, concentration, memory, organisation and imagination. Specially designed educational toys and games can therefore be used to stimulate learning in particular ways.

▼ Design for a board game

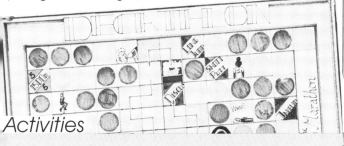

## Activities

1. Make a study of the suitability of ordinary toys and games for use by disabled children. Design a simple mechanical or electronic toy which will help a partially-sighted child to learn about colour, shape or pattern.
2. Choose an appropriate theme and design a board game which has an average play time of no more than twenty minutes. Test a series of prototypes and record the results. If possible include designs for three-dimensional playing pieces made from card, together with a very visually presented set of rules. Make suggestions for packaging and advertising.
3. Select an existing play space in your home or neighbourhood (anything from a 'play house' to an adventure playground). Critically study it and prepare detailed proposals for improvements, considering the needs of the very young or those who are handicapped in some way.

▲ Model of an electronic toy to help children learning counting, called SPEAKABACK.

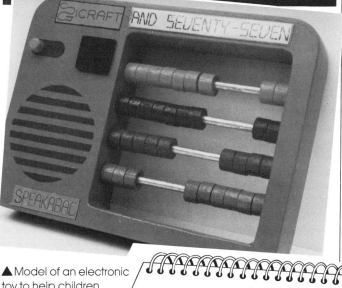

STARTING QUESTIONS

- What age range is the toy or game for?
- What are the most popular themes to use?
- How will it be 'educational'?
- What are the necessary safety standards?
- How much should it cost?

New materials and manufacturing technologies have opened up a wide range of new possibilities for fashion, and domestic product designers. There is now a great opportunity for designers to create radical new designs.

With just a few exceptions, however, most items of furniture available in High Street shops remain traditional and unadventurous, usually being cheaper copies of conventional designs already on the market.

There is, therefore, plenty of scope for the development of imaginative and exciting chairs, tables, storage units and so on which utilise modern materials and production methods. There is no reason why contemporary designs should not be as functional, comfortable and durable as traditional styles.

In the activities below you are not expected to construct full-size pieces of furniture. However, there are plenty of opportunities to develop ideas through prototypes, mock-ups and drawings, and to communicate by means of accurate scale presentation models and workshop plans.

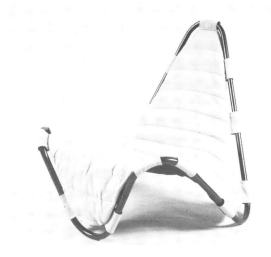

CHILDRENS CHAIR
SCALE 1·5
ALL DIMENSIONS IN MM

CARDBOARD TUBES LASHED TOGETHER WITH ROPE AND GLUED

MATERIALS:
CARDBOARD TUBES 110 Ø
CORRUGATED CARDBOARD BACKED FOAM (40MM THICK)
HESSIAN SACKING
THIN ROPE FOR LASHING TUBES TOGETHER

▲ Leaf chair

## Activities

1. Undertake a series of user tests on a range of different types of 'devices for sitting on' which you have at home. Make a comparative analysis of the use of materials, the construction, the finish, the appearance, the size and the cost. Present your study by means of a series of annotated drawings using various graphic conventions and techniques.

2. Use scrap packaging materials to produce at least two items of furniture for a teenager's room. As well as presentation drawings and models include a set of self-explanatory constructional drawings to illustrate the process of assembly of your designs.

3. Design an item of furniture for a particular person whom you know. The unit must be of specific use to the person and in some way reflect their personality and character.

4. Design a range of folding furniture suitable for use on a camping or caravan holiday. The items must be cheap to mass produce. Design a suitable package for each item, which can also be used for promotional display purposes.

## STARTING QUESTIONS

- What is the primary function of the unit?
- Does it serve any other purposes?
- What size should it be?
- What materials would be most suitable?
- Does it need to be sturdy?
- Does it need to be lightweight?

▲ Desk and chair made from scrap materials

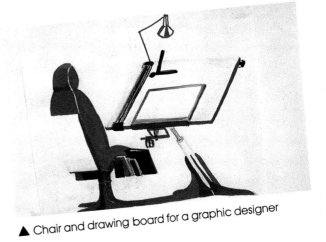

▲ Chair and drawing board for a graphic designer

▲ Chair for a specific person – a strong elder brother

▲ Chair for a designer who is also a heavy smoker

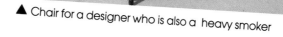

▲ Dining table　　　　▲ Occasional table　　　　▲ Dining table

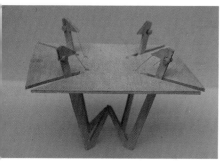

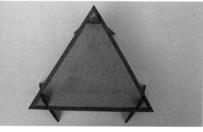

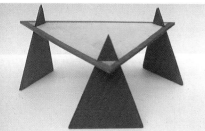

▲ Four views of a triangular dining table

## Activity

Look carefully at each of these models of ideas for items of furniture. For each design list the materials you consider potentially suitable for its construction.

Evaluate each design by giving your comments on:
- the proposed function;
- stability;
- ease of construction;
- visual appeal.

What methods could you use to test the proposed size of each item?

Each of the illustrations on these two pages is typical of the sort of drawings and constructions which might be produced to help develop, evaluate and communicate design ideas. They are all useful as part of your CDT Design and Communication course.

> **6** *In every design project you tackle, you will need to present your ideas to a client or colleague. If you can communicate your design ideas well to others, you are also better equipped to communicate them to yourself. The more a designer exercises these skills, the better he or she will become at visualising and understanding ideas as they develop.* **9**

Dick Powell

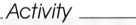

▲ Illustration for promotional graphic material for a new 'fun food' chain of restaurants

## Activity

For each illustration state:
 **(i)** If the designer has changed the **scale**, the **material** and/or the **form** of the model used (look back at pages 12 and 13).
 **(ii)** Which graphic media and/or materials have been used.
 **(iii)** How effective you think the use of colour and texture has been.

▲ Title graphics for a television series

▼ Preparatory drawings for a summer jacket. The final realisation (right) is worn by its designer

# DEVELOPMENT

POCKETS

PATTERN PIECES AND CONSTRUCTION

▲ Final presentation working model of the Bett box

▲▲ Large scale prototype mechanism
Final presentation model

▲ Ideas for graphic designs for the outside of a pill-box dispenser.

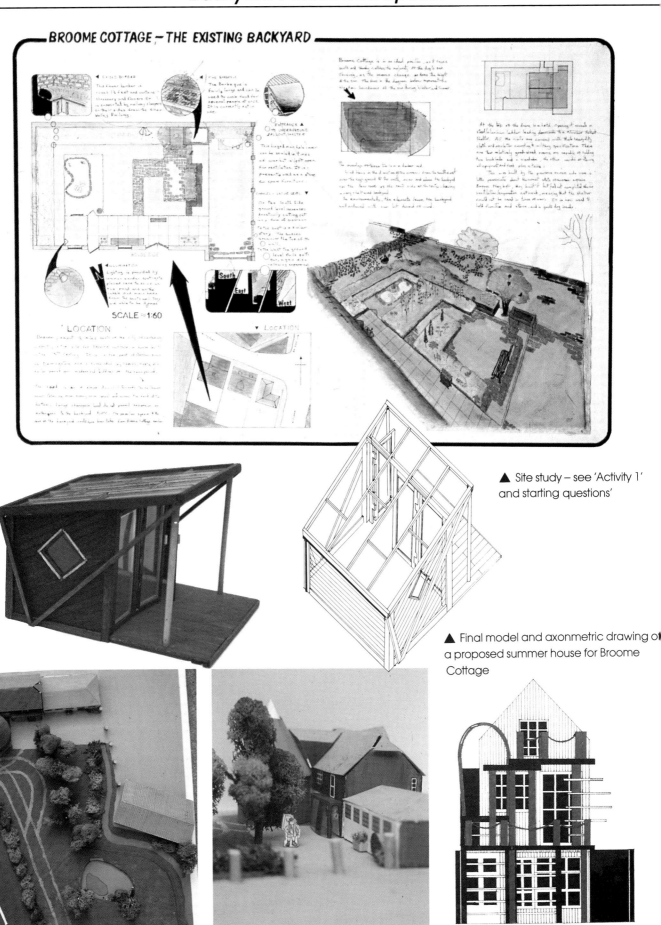

▲ Site study – see 'Activity 1' and starting questions'

▲ Final model and axonmetric drawing of a proposed summer house for Broome Cottage

▲ Model to show re-development of dis-used farmyard area

▲ Elevation showing terraced extention into a backyard space

Neglected backyard spaces are an excellent starting point for project work. Ideally the area should be immediately beside the building it belongs to and be reached through a direct door. You might find some examples in the following places:

- small gardens or back yards to terraced houses;
- small spaces in bigger gardens;
- disused plots of waste-land.

In making design proposals for re-developing the site, you must strike a balance between aesthetic factors (like visual and spatial attractiveness) and economic and technical factors (like foundations and drainage).

▲ A study of natural and man-made textured surfaces found in a backyard/garden area. Make a list of all the different surfaces which have been represented, and try the drawing technique used yourself.

## Activities

1. Using annotated sketches and diagrams, make a visual record of a neglected space in your locality – near your home or perhaps near your school. Try to find out how the space came to be as it is.

2. Present a series of design ideas for improvements to the space, bearing in mind some of the following points:
   - the light at different times of day
   - type of soil, trees, plants and flowers
   - location, orientation and prevailing winds
   - wildlife
   - garden furniture or fittings.

3. Prepare a *Which?*-style report for a particular item of backyard or garden equipment (shed, greenhouse, paving slab, pond and so on). Present the features of the various brands in a visual manner.

4. Research the possibilities and limitations of murals for wall decoration. Produce a mural design for a specific wall or fence.

STARTING QUESTIONS
SITE STUDY

- What materials have been used?
- What textures, colours and patterns are there?
- How is the space used?
- What is the light quality?
- What is the surrounding environment like?

# Packaging and Containers

A great many design problems are concerned with **containing** things which are:

- perishable – like food, drink, people and livestock
- dangerous – like chemicals and drugs
- precious – like money, documents and jewellery
- numerous – like marbles, pencils and stamps.

Usually these items are being contained because they need to be:

- stored safely until needed
- quickly identified
- easy to transport
- protected
- made accessible.

Drink cartons, crisp packets, clothes and handbags are just a few examples of containers. On a much larger scale, cars, aeroplanes and buildings contain people, who are perishable, precious and frequently numerous.

The design of a container has to be carefully matched to the situation and environment in which it will be used, and visual clues are needed to help identify its contents and how to open and close it.

Investigation: Methods of opening containers.

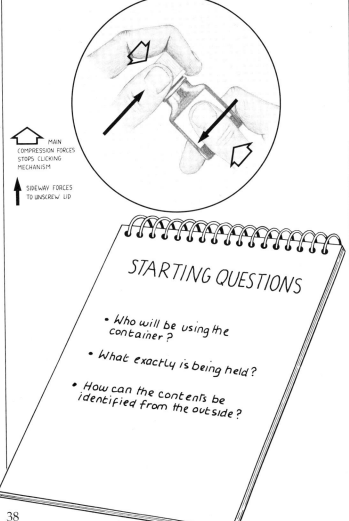

MAIN COMPRESSION FORCES STOPS CLICKING MECHANISM

SIDEWAY FORCES TO UNSCREW LID

## STARTING QUESTIONS

- Who will be using the container?
- What exactly is being held?
- How can the contents be identified from the outside?

## Activities

1. Make a list of the personal items that you (or someone you know well) carry around with you – particularly on holiday or for a hobby or leisure activity. Design an original means of carrying them so that they will be secure, yet available as necessary.

2. Design and make either a money box or a jewellery container. In either case, build in a secret opening mechanism, and produce an instruction sheet to explain how the mechanism works. You might like to consider how the external appearance of the box could use graphics to identify the contents.

3. Design a re-usable container for one or more disc-shaped pill(s). The device is for use by patients with certain medical conditions which require them to carry pills with them at all times in case of emergency.

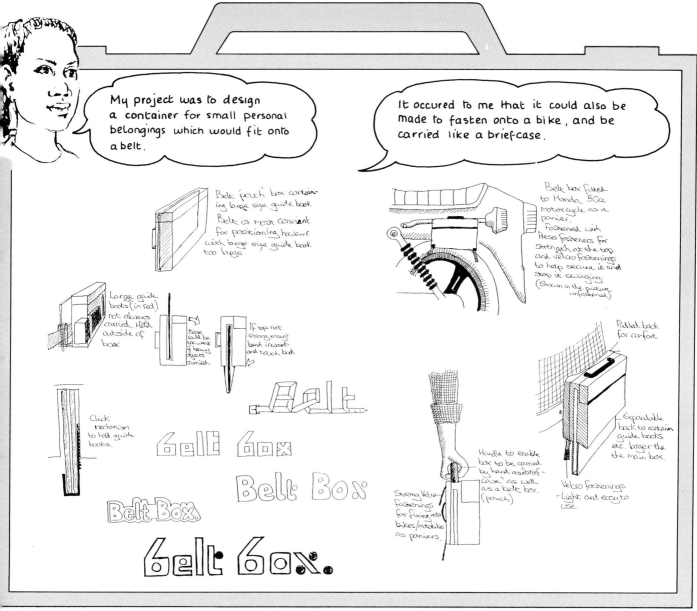

My project was to design a container for small personal belongings which would fit onto a belt.

It occured to me that it could also be made to fasten onto a bike, and be carried like a brief-case.

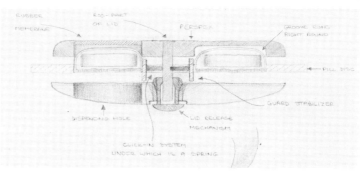

I talked to my sister who is a nurse and she told me these pill boxes must be quick and easy to open. Because they always have to be available and obvious (possibly even to passers-by who may need to help) they must look attractive so that they can be worn externally.

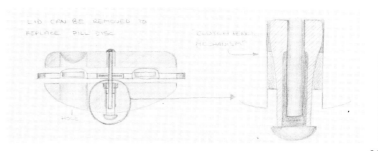

I eventually made a 3-D prototype, three times full size, so that the mechanism was easier to make. I also did some graphics for the outside to make the access disc easy to identify.

# One-room Living

There are many situations in which people live or work in small or confined spaces. Student accommodation, flats for the elderly, caravans and boats are common examples.

In these circumstances it is essential to arrange the furniture and fittings to make maximum use of the available space and still have everything accessible. Adequate safety, heating, lighting and ventilation are also essential.

Purely functional solutions to such problems are not enough, however. People also need their surroundings to be cheerful and friendly – with pleasant views, feelings of spaciousness, privacy and security. Living spaces need personal, individual touches – people need to feel 'at home'.

In the following projects you can explore a wide range of 2D and 3D modelling techniques to develop and communicate your solutions to living in confined spaces. Plan drawings on their own would not be nearly enough to give a real impression of how the space would look and feel.

## Activities

1. Select an existing room with area between 12 m$^2$ and 20 m$^2$ in a house you know and have access to. Show how it could be realistically converted into a self-contained unit for use either by a student or an elderly or handicapped person. Choose one of the following and produce detailed designs for it:
   - an item of furniture for the room
   - an automatic control system (e.g. for a security device)
   - a small range of co-ordinated fabric designs for the room.
2. Identify a youth club, sports or leisure complex in your area which has poor refreshment facilities. Produce design proposals for a coffee bar area.
3. Investigate the sources of information in a nearby tourist location. Develop design ideas for an appropriate static or mobile tourist information centre or kiosk.

4. Design a range of mass-produced fittings for use in bedrooms and self-catering apartments owned by a nationwide chain of hotels and holiday homes.

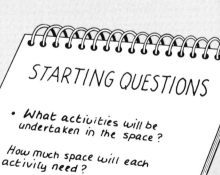

STARTING QUESTIONS

- What activities will be undertaken in the space?
- How much space will each activity need?
- How can the space be divided up?
- What scope is there for the user to personalise the space?

For this project I imagined that my grandfather (who is 73 years old) would move in with us. He is still active and proud of his independence, and would need a self-contained flatlet.

I designed some special fittings to convert existing kitchen cupboards so that they could house removable storage trays.

I began by looking at a simple layout using plans and later used a simple computer program to move things around.

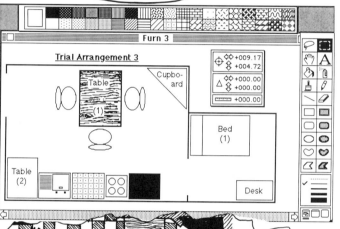

The project has renewed our family discussions about the possibility of my grandfather moving in with us.

# Putting on a Show

There are often times when people want to publicise ideas or information by putting on an exhibition or display. Some reasons for the display might be:

- to announce and promote a new product
- to present an account of a historical event
- to present works of art or craft
- for a fund-raising charity show.

Sometimes these exhibitions will be permanent, but generally they will be temporary and need to be transported to various locations.

Display systems for these travelling exhibitions have to be as flexible as possible to accommodate a wide range of exhibition sizes, types and locations. It is also important for the display to make the best possible use of light, colour and other visual elements that will add to its appeal.

## Activities

1. Assume that your school is planning to purchase a new system of display screens for temporary exhibitions of art and design work, parents' evenings and so on. Produce a *Which?*-style comparative analysis of the features, qualities and costs of existing systems on the market. Make a visually-based presentation report of your recommended purchase. Where can it be stored when it is not in use?

2. Choose a local venue which you consider suitable for conversion into a centre for temporary exhibitions. Present a series of plans, elevations, site-drawings and so on to show how the venue would need to be altered.

3. Make a study of the different types and effectiveness of shop-window displays. Choose a shop which you know well and design a window display for it based on a particular theme (like Christmas or summer holidays). Your final presentation should include a scale card model as well as instructions for the construction and installation of the window display.

4. A local manufacturing company wishes to construct fifty free-standing point-of-sale structures to provide display space for a new range of potato crisps. They are to be used in newsagents and sweet shops. Produce scale card models of three different sized structures for use in confined situations.

### STARTING QUESTIONS

- Where will the display be?

- What is it about?

- How much material is there to display?

- How can the display be changed or moved?

- What information will the public need?

The main part of my project was to re-design the interior of our local village hall so that it could be used for small displays as well as social functions. I also had to produce a brochure to attract support and sponsorship for the venture. I made a tape and slide sequence based on a series of card models.

**Information design** is concerned with developing two-dimensional graphic work to provide ideas or information. Record sleeves, magazines, sign systems, posters, timetables and instruction leaflets are typical products in this area.

Such work needs to be readily understood and must give the information quickly, clearly and unambiguously. Often, especially when the message is intended to sell or promote something, visual images are used to make a product seem extremely desirable. At other times the message needs to be memorable, and there are a number of devices that designers use to make messages more memorable:

- make it strange or puzzling
- distort its proportions
- make it dynamic (i.e. make it carry out an action)
- exaggerate the number
- make it brilliantly coloured.

Make a collection of brochures, record sleeves, and book jackets which show an effective use of such devices. What have the designers done for the cover of this book to add to its appeal?

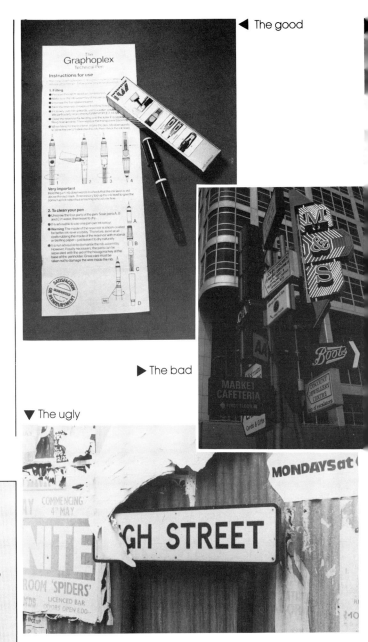

◄ The good

► The bad

▼ The ugly

## Activities

1. Design and produce the artwork for a poster for one of the following:
   - a local festival or fête
   - road safety in your neighbourhood
   - discouraging teenagers from starting to smoke, drink or experiment with drugs.

2. Choose a locally-based organisation that is trying to raise money for a good cause. Devise and present a varied campaign to attract public attention and increase support.

3. Find examples of a selection of the following instruction sheets:
   - self-assembly furniture
   - making an item of clothing
   - operating an electronic device (such as a video recorder).
   Evaluate each and comment on the effectiveness of the communication. Re-design one of them for use by someone with reading difficulties.

4. Design and produce the artwork for a brochure for one of the following:
   - a local tourist attraction
   - a recent design of yours – or one produced by someone else in your school.

*STARTING QUESTIONS*

- Who is the information aimed at?
- What is the essential message?
- How can I make it noticeable?
- Where will it be seen?

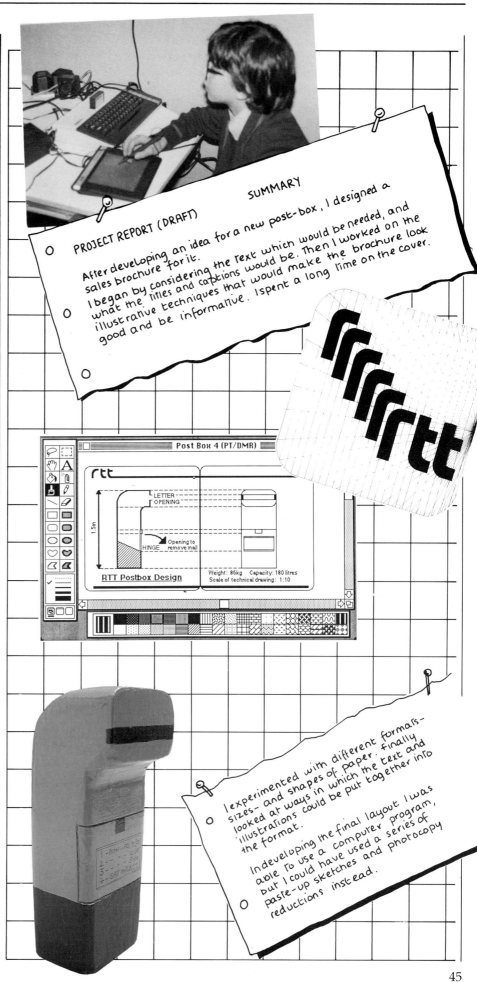

PROJECT REPORT (DRAFT)

SUMMARY

After developing an idea for a new post-box, I designed a sales brochure for it.

I began by considering the text which would be needed, and what the titles and captions would be. Then I worked on the illustrative techniques that would make the brochure look good and be informative. I spent a long time on the cover.

Post Box 4 (PT/DMR)

rtt

LETTER OPENING

1.5m

HINGE   Opening to remove mail

RTT Postbox Design

Weight: 85kg    Capacity: 180 litres
Scale of technical drawing: 1:10

I experimented with different formats – sizes and shapes of paper. Finally I looked at ways in which the text and illustrations could be put together into the format.

In developing the final layout I was able to use a computer program, but I could have used a series of paste-up sketches and photocopy reductions instead.

45

# Corporate Identity Systems

Organisations, both large and small, usually try to present themselves to their customers and employees in a unified and consistent manner. One way of achieving this is to use a co-ordinated range of graphic symbols, layout, colour and type-style on their products and letter heads. The **corporate identity** provides a quick and easily recognised way of labelling products and services, and helps to reinforce public awareness of them.

In some cases, corporate identity systems might involve little more than a logo or symbol that can be used on a letter head or business card. At the other extreme a large national or global organisation might use a large number of subtle variations on the basic design so as to relate all the aspects of their business. Packaging, products, instruction leaflets, invoices, advertisements, uniforms, delivery vans, carrier bags and retail outlets can thus be unified under the banner of the corporation.

## Activities

1. Make a collection of commercial visual identity logos and symbols. Group them under the headings:
   - Initial letters
   - Whole name
   - Product illustration.

   What qualities do they portray – efficiency, tradition, high-tech, durability, speed?

2. Make a study of your school uniform, or one of a nearby school. Why is it the way it is? What do pupils and staff think of it? Present a series of designs for a new visual identity for the school, involving a uniform and other graphic items.

3. Obtain some examples of graphic work used by an existing international corporation, and compare them with what is used by a small local business. Try to talk to representatives of the companies to find out how the system was developed, and what they think of it.

4. Present a folio of design work, for a new chain of either fast-food or health-food restaurants and take-aways. The company is regionally based and this must be reflected in your proposals.

Choose a possible site for the restaurant or take-away and produce:
   - a site location drawing
   - an internal layout drawing
   - street elevations of the shop front
   - a pictorial drawing of part of the interior
   - a range of packaging, paper-ware, menus, uniforms, signs and promotional material.

### STARTING QUESTIONS

- What product or service is being sold?

- Which items could be unified with a visual identity system?

- What are the needs of the employees?

- How effective is the present system?

I visited a new microcomputer shop and noticed that they did not have a visual identity scheme. The manager said he would be interested to see any ideas I could come up with.

I experimented with lots of ideas for the basic logo. I used my sketchbook and a simple computer program.

I produced a detailed and fully-dimensional drawing of the final proposal, and made up samples of letter heads and other possible uses of the logo.

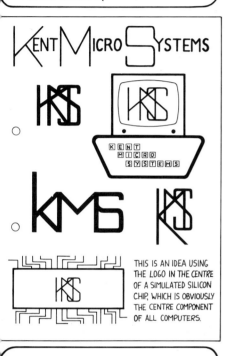

THIS IS AN IDEA USING THE LOGO IN THE CENTRE OF A SIMULATED SILICON CHIP, WHICH IS OBVIOUSLY THE CENTRE COMPONENT OF ALL COMPUTERS.

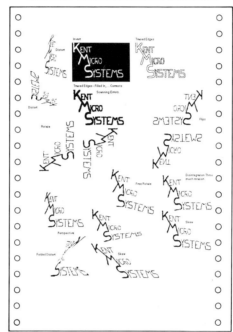

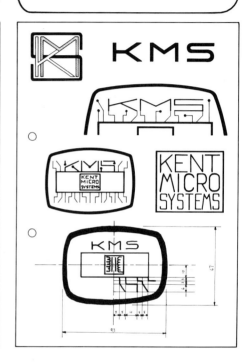

I put the samples together into a folder and sent them to the manager – who rang me to say how impressed he was.

Paper and card are cheap and versatile materials which can be used in many (often surprising) ways. They can easily be cut, bent, folded, printed on and joined, and are used extensively for packaging and for 'pop-up' books and greetings cards.

Paper engineering for these purposes dates back to Victorian times, although the basic principles can be discovered in the ancient Japanese craft of origami.

A paper kit model of the new Lloyd's building

## Activities

1. Collect some recent examples of pop-up books and cards. Examine them closely to discover how the mechanisms work. Use scrap card to make up some of the mechanisms yourself. Using the principles you have discovered, design a series of greetings cards.

2. Design and make a pop-up book with three inside double pages and a back and front cover. The book should be designed for children aged between 5 and 8 years, and can either be factual or be a simple short story based on a theme of your choice (such as the 'Transformers' cartoon).

3. Make and present a study of the ways in which packaging is used for protection during transportation. Look particularly at construction, resulting strength and the graphic presentation.

4. Select one of the following and design a suitable package for it:
   - a craft knife with spare blades
   - two light bulbs
   - three cotton reels of different colours
   - four small cream cakes
   - 100 drinking straws.

You may use other materials as well as card if necessary. Pay particular attention to the graphics, and include appropriate information and instructions for use or storage.

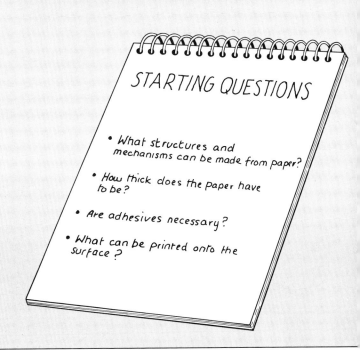

STARTING QUESTIONS

- What structures and mechanisms can be made from paper?

- How thick does the paper have to be?

- Are adhesives necessary?

- What can be printed onto the surface?

For my Pop-up book I talked to our neighbour's young son, and found some good pictures and text in the Library. I had to make and test many prototypes before I achieved the effects I wanted.

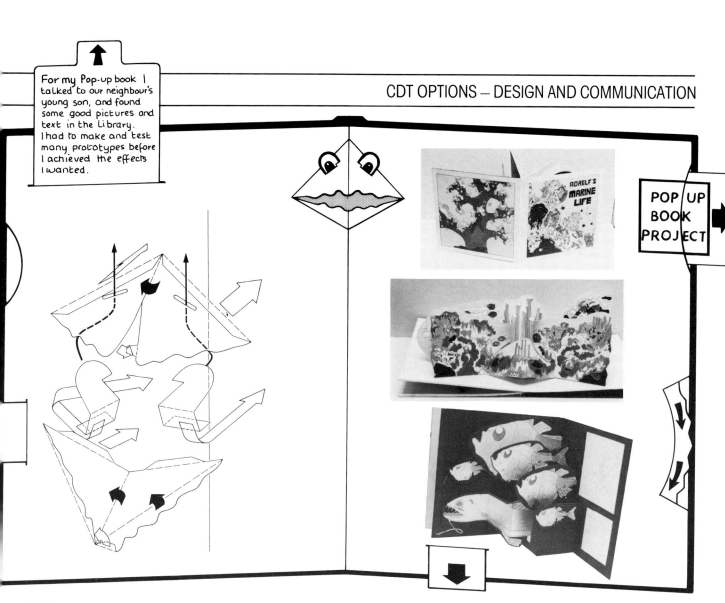

POP UP BOOK PROJECT

ADRELF'S MARINE LIFE

I visited a baker's shop to find out about problems of folding cake-boxes up. I went back to test out my prototypes. Finally I added appropriate graphics to the outside of the box.

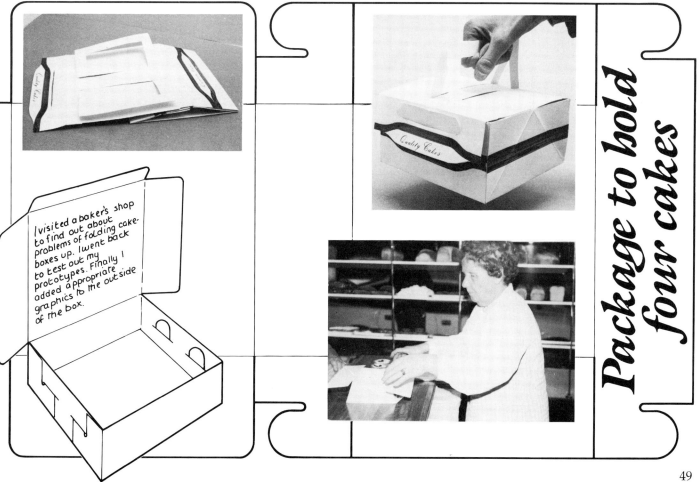

Quality Cakes

Package to hold four cakes

There are many different types of robot and robotic devices, ranging from space probes to medical simulators or toys. In one way or another they all attempt to substitute for a human being.

Designing and making such machines is a very complex business involving detailed technical matters like energy sources, mechanical components, control systems and so on. It is also useful to understand how human sensory and biological systems work.

Beyond all the technical aspects are moral, social and psychological considerations. Questions you could ask are:

- Which jobs should robots be allowed to do at the expense of people's livelihoods?
- What should robots look like to make them acceptable to us?
- In what situations is the 'personal touch' essential?

Although you are unlikely to be building a robot as part of your Design and Communication course, there are plenty of interesting projects that you can do in this area.

Collage of a robot

## Activities

1. Produce an illustrated study pack for 8 to 11 year-old school children entitled 'The future of robots'. Use a mixture of text, diagrams, technical illustrations and cartoons to portray your vision of how robotic devices will affect the home or the office of the future. Your predictions must be based on some evidence of the technological possibilities, and should not be simply a fantasy. Think about the time scale of your predictions – is it 10, 20, 50 or 100 years from now?

2. Make a study of simple robotic-type devices which are currently available and reasonably cheap to buy. Consider the domestic needs of handicapped or elderly people and identify potential uses for such devices in the home (possibly involving some modifications). Present your findings visually and in such a way that the potential user would not be alarmed at your proposal.

## STARTING QUESTIONS

- What are the technological capabilities of robots at the moment?

- Where are they most often used?

- What tasks are they most suitable for?

- Does it matter what a robot looks like?

- What makes a robot better or worse (or just different) than a human being?

▲ A cartoon from a pupil's project which studied the advantages and disadvantages of using robots instead of human beings

## Graphics Techniques

### Elevations

Elevations describe the vertical planes of objects – their fronts, sides and backs – and reveal arrangements of components and their surroundings.

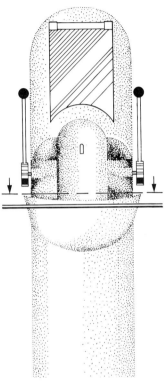

▲ Wash-basin/sink unit.

### Orthographic projections

Plans and elevations on their own are poor at showing 3D appearance and details. Used together, however, they can provide a great deal of information, providing the reader understands the conventions of first and third angle projection.

### General assembly (Production workshop) drawings

When a drawing is intended as a precise specification for workshop assembly, a general assembly drawing gives full information about overall dimensions, materials and assembly of components. Separate detailed drawings in orthographic projection are then provided for each component.

### Isometric projections (30°)

Isometric projections provide a quick and easy method of discovering what an object will look like in three dimensions. They can be used in rough sketch form to help develop ideas, or can be accurately measured up from scale plans and elevations.

### Axonometric drawings (45°)

Axonometric drawings are usually used for drawings of buildings or spaces. Circular forms are very easy to draw.

### Planometric or oblique drawings

An alternative system which can be drawn straight off a plan.

### Perspective

Drawings in perspective give a realistic illusion of depth, which is very easy for the reader to understand. One-point perspective is fairly easy to draw, and useful in developmental sketches. It is less effective than two- and three-point perspective which can be very difficult to draw accurately to scale.

### Exploded views

Three-dimensional drawings can be **exploded** to provide greater clarity of the way in which various components fit together. They are very useful for illustrating an assembly procedure.

### Cross-sections

A cross-section is usually an elevation of an object or building drawn as if a slice has been cut through part or all of it, revealing information about the inside of the structure.

### Cut-aways

Similar to the cross-section, the cut-away removes the outer portions of an enclosed object or space to reveal more about its interior.

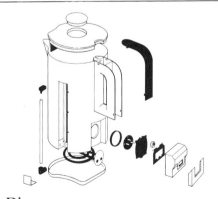

### Diagrams

Diagrams are most effective for representing numerical information, spatial relationships and operational sequences. There are many different types of diagram: flow-diagrams; networks; matrices; graphs; bar charts; pie charts and histograms to name a few.

### Rendering

You can use colour; texture; shading; shadows and reflections in order to provide visual impact, emphasise or code various components, provide realism by providing information about the look and feel of the surfaces of materials, make objects look more solid, give a greater illusion of depth.

## Maps and plans
Maps and plans show the spatial locations of components of objects or places in relationship to each other from an imaginary 'bird's eye' viewpoint.

## Scales
Standard scales are 1:200, 1:100, 1:50, 1:20, 1:5 and 1:2 (that is, half size). Choose which to use according to the size of the object being drawn, the amount of detail to be shown and the size of the paper you are using. A scale of 2:1 means twice full size.

## Visual presentation devices
The following can all be used to present ideas and information in a lively way so as to attract attention and sustain interest: cartoons, storyboards, animatics, overlays, photomontages, collages, low-relief models and 3D representations.

## Graphic symbols
Graphic symbols provide information visually and are often used to identify, direct, warn and so on.

## Geometry
You need to know how to construct and calculate geometric solids, areas, tangents, loci, ellipses, auxillary views, interpenetrations and surface developments.

## Media checklist
**Pencils** – 9H to 6B lead-coloured leads
**Pens** – fountain, technical, ruling, graphos, felt markers, ball-points

**Permanent inks** – Indian black or coloured
**Paint** – powder, water colour, designers' gouache, PVA, oils, aerosol sprays

**Chalks**
**Charcoal**
**Crayons** – wax or 'Conte'
**Pre-coloured surfaces** – card, paper, tape, plastic, films, printed papers

**Paper** – select from the following according to weight, texture, colour and opaqueness:
newsprint, detail or layout, cartridge, off-set bond, manilla sugar, tracing, tracing film, card, cardboard and many other specialist papers suitable for different paints and inks
**Stencils** – lettering, symbols, flexicurves, other drawing aids
**Photo-mechanical** – photo-copier, diazo (die-line)
**Photographic** – black and white or colour prints, slide or movie film
**Electronic** – video, computer generation (VDU or print-out)

Your work for Design and Communication will also involve an awareness of the following areas, more details of which are to be found in other sections of this book.

1. **Designing, making and evaluating** – as outlined in the Common Core section.

2. **Design and communication in society** – the social, economic, political and moral values relating to the past, the present and the future.

3. **Materials** – different *types*, such as woods, metals, and plastics and, for model-making, polystyrenes, foam, plasticine, paper, card, fabrics, ceramics and so on.
   Different *qualities* and *working characteristics*, such as mechanical, thermal, electrical, structural and manipulative.
   Associated *manufacturing* and *fabrication technologies*, such as finishing, forming, shaping and joining components.

4. **Technology**
   *i) Control systems*
   Static – fastenings and fittings
       – bearings
       – forces and structures

   Dynamic – eccentric, cams and followers, gears, belts, chains, pulleys, levers, shafts, motors, elastic bands

   *ii) Energy* – control, conversion and transmission
       – sources
       – types
       – storage

An important part of your final coursework assessment is the presentation of a folio of project work. You may be asked to put up a display of your work, and possibly have to discuss it with a visiting examiner.

You should tackle the presentation of your work just as you would any other design problem. You must undertake some investigation and detailed research and should consider a number of different approaches and ideas. You should also remember to allocate plenty of time for the preparation, mounting etc. of your work.

Just as you need to look well-turned out for a job or college interview, so your work needs to be carefully presented too. First impressions are always very important.

### What material needs to be included?
The short answer is – virtually everything. Use the following checklist to ensure that you are including as much as possible of appropriate material in each project that you submit for assessment.

You will find it very helpful if you do a series of preparatory sketches like these to help plan the presentation of your work.

Experiment with enlarging and reducing the sizes of areas of text and illustrations to achieve a good balance of space and material.

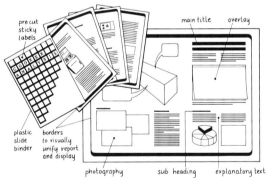

### Presenting a project report
● What will the cover be like?
● What sequence will the contents be presented in?
● How will the text and illustrations be integrated?
● Will it be typed out?
● How wide should the margins be?
● What format will it be?
● How will it be bound together?

### Planning presentation/display panels
● Is there a good mixture of text and illustrative material?
● Is it clear which illustrations relate to which sections of text?

● Sketchbooks and notebooks recording the full development of your ideas.
● Evidence of prototypes that you have made, the prototypes themselves and records of how you tested and evaluated them.
● A final report documenting and evaluating your project as a whole.
● Display panels to clearly explain the problem you tackled and what your proposed solutions are.
● Final models and supporting technical graphics, representing your 'realisation', along with any relevant tape/slide, film or video sequences.
● Yourself – prepare a clear sequential spoken account of the development of the project, making as much direct reference as possible to the material on display.

● Which grid lines can you use to visually tie the panel together?
● Can you use space to separate different sections, rather than drawing lines or boxes?
● How can you use colour most effectively?
● How many panels will there be?
● What size paper or card will you use?

# Examination Checklist

These tables are a rough guide to the different patterns of coursework assessment and examination papers required by each of the GCSE Examining Groups. You should ask your teacher for more precise details of any particular syllabus or area of a syllabus.

| | % | Term 1 | Term 2 | Term 3 | Term 4 | Term 5 | June Exams |
|---|---|---|---|---|---|---|---|
| **LONDON AND EAST ANGLIAN GROUP** | | | | | | | |
| Coursework (1)   General | 25 | ← | → | ← | → | | |
| Coursework (2)   Mini-project | 15 | | | ←→ | | | |
| Paper 2   Design Assignment | 30 | | | | ← | → | |
| Paper 1   Common Core/ Specialist Areas | 30 | | | | | | 2½ hrs |
| | | | | | | | |
| **MIDLAND EXAMINING GROUP** | | | | | | | |
| Coursework (1)   Mini-project | 15 | | ← | → | | | |
| Coursework (2)   Major-project | 25 | | | | ← | → | |
| Paper 1   Common Core | 35 | | | | | | 2¼ hrs |
| Paper 2-4   Specialist Areas | 25 | | | | | | 2¼ hrs |
| | | | | | | | |
| **NORTHERN EXAMINING ASSOCIATION** | | | | | | | |
| Coursework   (2 best topics) | 40 | ← | | | | → | |
| Design Assignment | 30 | | | | ← | → | |
| Paper 1   Common Core | 30 | | | | | | 2½ hrs |
| | | | | | | | |
| **SOUTHERN EXAMINING GROUP** | | | | | | | |
| Coursework | 50 | | | | ← | → | |
| Paper 1   Common Core | 20 | | | | | | 1¾ hrs |
| Paper 2   Design Situations | 30 | | | | | | 2 hrs |
| | | | | | | | |
| **WELSH JOINT EDUCATION COMMITTEE** | | | | | | | |
| Coursework   (Major Project) | 30 | | | | ← | → | |
| Paper 1   General | 30 | | | | | | 2 hrs |
| Paper 2   General, plus specialist options | 40 | | | | | | 2½ hrs |

# CDT
## OPTIONS ▶ *DESIGN AND REALISATION*

In this course, you will build on your experience of designing, making and evaluating that we outlined in the section on the common core. The emphasis of the course is on practical design situations that will require you to produce products (using materials and tools) that solve people's problems.

Designed by Paul Stead

Look at this piece of furniture that has been designed for an executive office. Think of the range of skills and experience that would be required to design and make it. You would have to:

- understand how materials behave – especially rigid materials like wood, metal and plastics
- have the skills to work the materials by hand or with suitable machinery
- understand all the safe working procedures, so as not to hurt yourself, or anyone else.

All these skills would help you to **make** the desk, but as we saw in the earlier sections, to **design** it would need an even larger range of skills.

You would need to understand what it was **required to do** by discussing it with your 'client'.

You would need to be able to **draw** and **model** a range of possibilities until your client was satisfied with the product.

You would need to make sensible **choices** for the materials and components. (This is discussed in detail on page 84.)

You would need to be able to **explain** your proposals thoroughly and clearly to the client.

You would need to explain to the manufacturer how you wanted it **produced**.

You would need to be able to do all of this **within the budget** that you agreed with your client.

This is the world of **product design**, and it is responsible for many of the items which we use in everyday life. In this course you will gain a greater understanding of the products used by human beings, and should be able to choose between those that work effectively and those that don't.

## Product analysis

This is a critical area of work in CDT. The investigation of commercially-produced products is an expanding business in its own right. *Which?*-type magazines on consumer products are easily acquired, and include *Which Car?*, *Which Computer?* and *Which Holiday?*.

Producing these reports requires very careful analysis of product function, and how it relates to cost, comfort and convenience. In your Design and Realisation course you will almost certainly have to do a number of product analysis exercises.

The work shown here was produced in response to a product analysis exercise concerning how a garden plant spray works.

Product analysis work of this kind will also enable you to think about wider issues of social responsibility. Should we use materials that are recycled – or should we continue to deplete the world's natural resources? Should we encourage design for minority groups such as for people suffering from particular handicaps, or leave things as they are?

This aspect of your work may provide you with a useful link with other school subjects, which you should regard as useful sources of information for many aspects of a Design and Realisation course.

## Product ergonomics

The vast majority of the products that make up the manufactured environment were produced for use by human beings. Logically, therefore, consideration must be given to the people who are likely to use the item, and how they relate to the sizes, shapes weights and other physical properties of the product. This study is called **ergonomics**. Most humans are very adaptable and can conform themselves to anything which suits their purposes. There are, however, limits which are beyond human endurance. Both the professional product designer and the pupil following a Design and Realisation course must be aware of the ergonomic aspects of product design.

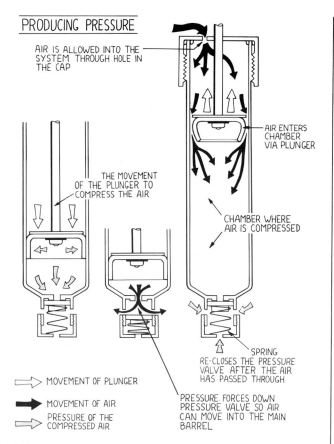

PRODUCING PRESSURE

AIR IS ALLOWED INTO THE SYSTEM THROUGH HOLE IN THE CAP

THE MOVEMENT OF THE PLUNGER TO COMPRESS THE AIR

AIR ENTERS CHAMBER VIA PLUNGER

CHAMBER WHERE AIR IS COMPRESSED

SPRING RE-CLOSES THE PRESSURE VALVE AFTER THE AIR HAS PASSED THROUGH

PRESSURE FORCES DOWN PRESSURE VALVE SO AIR CAN MOVE INTO THE MAIN BARREL

⇨ MOVEMENT OF PLUNGER

➡ MOVEMENT OF AIR

⇨ PRESSURE OF THE COMPRESSED AIR

Analysis of the functioning of a garden plant spray

This part of the book illustrates a range of themes that are suitable for Design and Realisation projects. Many of the products illustrated have been produced by pupils in the 4th and 5th year of school. Some of these projects were decided upon by the teacher. Others were thought up entirely by an individual pupil or a group of pupils.

Can you see your own interests catered for by one or more of these themes? If not, then you should start working some out for yourself. You may find that the questions in the text, and the activities that are listed on each page, will help you to work out some of your own ideas.

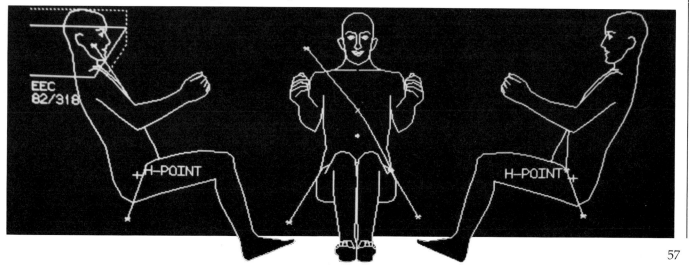

EEC 82/318

H-POINT

H-POINT

# Containers and Storage

The need to **contain** or **house** objects is a common source of design problems. This type of problem is suitable for your Design and Realisation studies for a number of reasons:

- the storage requirements are usually quite specific (like where does it go, what does it contain) and are easy to research
- a wide range of containers is possible, offering plenty of scope for your designing
- the range of materials for the realisation is very wide.

## Think about function

Nicholas designed and made a box for containing his modelling tools and equipment. He wanted the container to hold many small items and needed them to be laid out clearly when he was in the middle of a project. In his final design each of the drawers was partitioned, and used to house specific items of equipment. The ergonomics of using this box were a very important part of the design. Can you suggest a way of making inserts for the inside of the drawers?

Lara wanted a stand for her record player, as she was forever falling over it on the floor. She was able to use the structure of her stand to contain her records and tapes. After having considered a number of ideas on paper it was a simple task to make up some scale models from cardboard to explore the ideas more thoroughly.

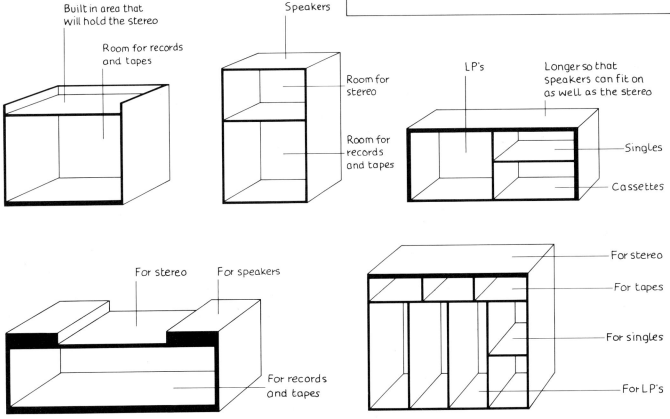

## Think about fittings, fixtures and construction

Lara chose mahogany-veneered chipboard for her stand. She investigated the use of knock-down fittings, but chose instead to use glue and chipboard screws to hold the joints together. Can you think of a disadvantage of using the plastic block type of knock-down fittings?

Anna's 'A' box was designed to be made in copper sheet, and this meant she had to get a lot of practice in joining techniques for sheet metal. How do you join together pieces of copper and similar materials? The harsh nature of sheet metal did not provide the sort of inner protection she wanted for her jewellery items, so the inside of the box had to be lined. What materials and techniques could she have used for this?

## Think about form

Both of the previous projects resulted in relatively simple and functional forms, but often the form of a container is its most important feature. Look at this range of simple containers which seem to have been designed to have very special forms.

Anna began her project by researching 'containerism' in a wide context. She had ideas for containers for small items of jewellery and knick-knacks which were both functional and decorative. Her final choice was to make a container based on the letter 'A'. Containers with special forms (like this one) are almost always more difficult to make than those designed simply to hold specific objects. Can you think of ways of making up the shape of this container or of fixing a lid onto the base piece?

Anna's 'A' box

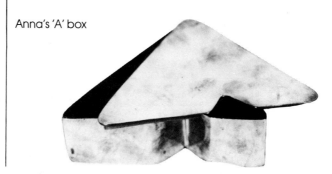

## Activities

1. Work out a way by which lengths of plastic drainpipe or other plastic plumbing material could be used to make a container with a lid. What sizes of tube are available? What sorts of thing would you need to store? How can you make a lid fit on?

2. Design and make a money box which includes a simple mechanism which is activated by the weight of a coin. Do you want to limit the size or type of coin that will go in? How big should the box be? What might the mechanism do? (See pages 68 and 69 for further ideas about this.)

3. Design and make a rack for a set of drawing equipment that you need for all your school work. Where should the rack be situated? Should it be portable so that you can take it to school when you need it? Should it be free standing?

# Lighting Up the Home

There are many uses for different types of lighting in and around the home. Some lighting needs to be direct and bright, whilst in other situations you need soft and indirect light. Look around your home and make a list of the places where these sorts of light are used.

Here are some ideas that might get you started. Pick a theme and then research the range of lighting that might exist within it. Try to think of situations where you need a particular sort of light and then design it for yourself.

- Lighting for **function** – in a garage or shed
- Lighting for **fun** – in your bedroom or the sitting room
- Lighting for **toddlers** – the two lighting units illustrated below were designed by 4th year pupils who had studied the problems of 'night lights' for toddlers
- Lighting for **atmosphere**
- Lighting for **style**

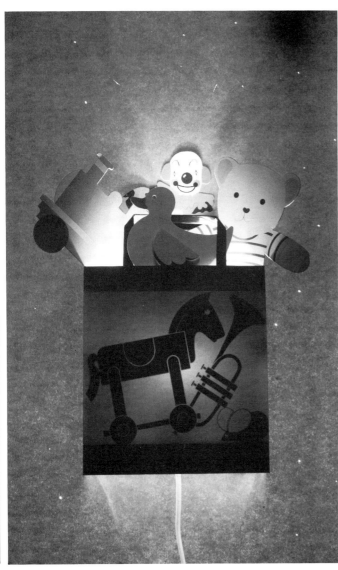

## Lightbulbs get hot

Many commercially-produced lighting units and fittings specify a maximum **wattage** for the bulb. This is an important consideration, as the bulb produces **heat** as well as light. You must allow for the heat to escape, but this problem can be used to good effect. Hot air rises, and the movement of the resulting convection current can be used to your advantage. Can you work out two ways of using the heat generated by a light bulb, one of which is purely decorative, the other purely functional?

## Electric lights can be dangerous

When designing a lighting unit, for whatever purpose, you have to consider certain safety features. This is particularly true if mains electricity is to be used as the power source. If you have to buy any fittings, you should ensure that they are correctly connected. If your design contains any metallic components they will need to be properly earthed. It would, in fact, be quite appropriate to have a qualified electrician check your connections for you. This would not take anything away from the authenticity of your project.

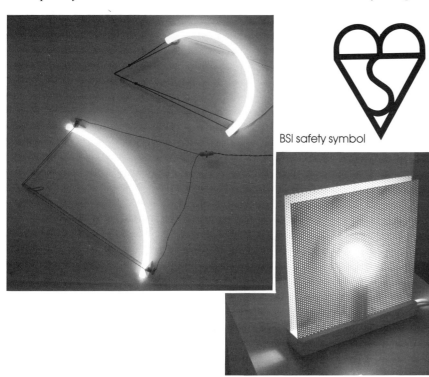

BSI safety symbol

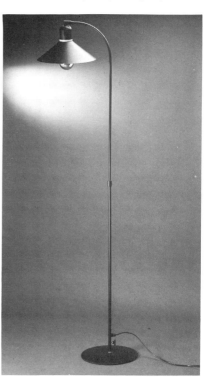

## Activities

1. Many young children are frightened by the dark and need some form of low-level lighting to be on all through the night in their bedroom. Design and make a lighting unit appropriate to this situation. What safety regulations apply to this problem? How bright should the light be? Should it be plain white light or coloured? Where can the light be fixed? What materials could you use?

2. Collect a range of lighting illustrations from magazines and catalogues. Organise them under headings that indicate the situations in which they would be used, and the functions that they perform. Study one in detail and try to work out the details of the materials it was made from, and the production techniques that were used.

3. Design and make a simple table-top lighting unit which is suitable for both direct and indirect lighting, according to the needs of the moment. Should the light be adjustable for direction (like an angle-poise lamp)? What are the surroundings like? What might the direct light be needed for?

4. Design and make a unit which will attach to the edge of an A2 drawing board to illuminate a drawing as it is produced. What sort of light source (e.g. fluorescent) will you use? What power does the light need? Should it be directional? Should it be detachable or fitted permanently onto the board?

5. Design and make a light unit that uses the heat from the bulb to create movement.

# Operational Devices

The title 'operational devices' covers a multitude of sins (and design opportunities). An operational device may have any function, and may be of use to anyone. They may be operational in and around the home, or be just what we need to carry in the boot of the car for some particular reason. They might be 'operated' by an animal in our back yard (for example, by tripping a wildlife-camera trigger). They may be mechanically operated, electrically powered or even electronically controlled.

Here is a range of themes that might be used to explore the notion of operational devices:
- Timers – to aid in the kitchen
- Counters – to instruct the milkman
- Hangers – for towels or hose pipes
- Animal operators – e.g. bird feeders
- Clampers – for letters or workshop operations
- Openers – for jars or bottles
- Crackers – for nuts.

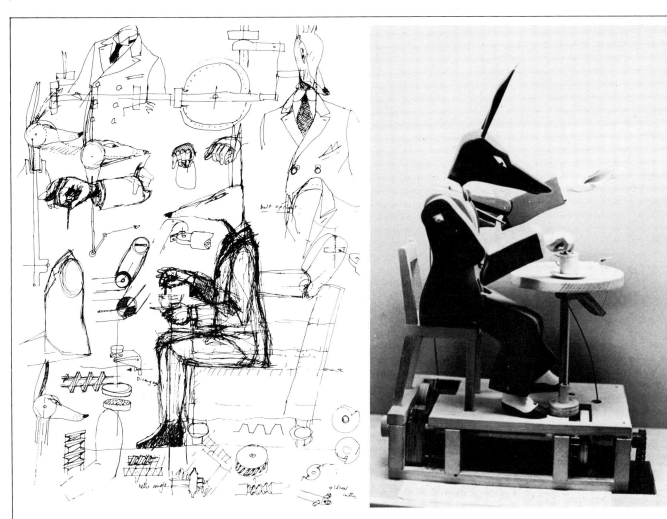

6 *Design sketches serve as a means of exploring thoughts. In as much as they are technical drawings, they are used to try out the practicality of an idea for a machine before the labour of modelmaking or prototype-making begins. When work has begun on a piece, I still keep drawing to check whether I've considered all the possible solutions. Even when I've finished a piece, I still make drawings to remind myself of what I've done, to feed into future projects.* 9

Paul Spooner

This type of designing is likely to involve you in producing a precise **technical specification** for the operational components. It will also involve the sort of detailed design sketches that are shown here. Working out the movement involved in the operation can be very tricky. You will probably start with sketches like these, and then move on to simple mechanical models.

Many people seem to enjoy eating fresh nuts. They are prepared to put time and effort into removing the outer shell from walnuts or brazil nuts, even though they could buy them without shells. It seems to be a particularly popular tradition at Christmas. Illustrated opposite are four examples of nutcrackers which were produced by a fourth year group.

Each of the pupils investigated the existing types of nutcracker that could be bought in the shops. They all rely on some form of mechanical operation. What are the basic mechanical principles used in most commercially-made nutcrackers? Many were found to need considerable strength to operate, and lacked any means of control. On many occasions the user was left picking pieces of shell out of the crushed remnants of the nut. How do these examples overcome this problem? How suitable do you think they are? How well do they tackle the problems of:

- ease of operation
- soundness of construction
- cleanability
- degree of control
- fun of using?

See if you can work out how each could be made.

### Devices for the handicapped

Any operational device that we use is likely to be more difficult for people who are handicapped in some way. If they can't see too well, or if their hands are damaged by arthritis, or if they find it difficult to move around freely, they will have problems. Imagine trying to put toothpaste onto a brush if you only have one hand, or trying to garden from a wheelchair.

Often the handicapped can benefit enormously from some simple modification to an existing product. But equally, there are times when their needs demand much more comprehensive design consideration. Talk to your teacher about the possibilities of doing a project such as this. It might be a good start to visit a local hospital and see for yourself some of the problems that have to be tackled.

## Activities

1. Design and make a foot-operated device which will hold a garage door or garden gate open in a strong breeze. Where could it be fixed? How might the release mechanism work?

2. Design and make a device to enable a wheelchair-bound table-tennis player to pick up a ball from the floor. What reach would be needed? Where can the device be fixed? How could it be operated? How often will it be needed?

3. Design a bird-table drinking-water device that keeps itself topped up with rainwater. What birds do you want to encourage to use your table? Can you make the device so that only those birds can use it? How can you channel the rainwater so that it keeps topped up but does not overflow and make a mess?

### Tables and draughting units

On this and the next double page, you will look at horizontal working surfaces – tables and draughting units. They can be very useful pieces of furniture. Do you have a single room in your house which does not have a table or work surface of some sort? We use them as permanent stands, as temporary stands or as surfaces on which to work, eat, read, build models, write books, do jig-saw puzzles and so on. They can be built into the house or be free standing. They can be solid or collapsible, fixed or adjustable. The variety of tables that exists reflects the diversity of tasks that people use them for and the range of styles that they find pleasing.

Illustrated here are some tables, designed for different purposes, made from different materials and using different construction methods.

You can see that the design of tables and working surfaces is a matter that requires careful thought about the **function** that the surface performs. This will involve you in a lot of research and discussion with your 'client'. Much of this research will be to do with ergonomics – that is, working out the exact sizes (height, width, area, length) that you need to have for the table to suit the people who are going to use it. Using sketches will only get you part of the way to a solution. You will almost certainly have to model your proposal to get a proper impression of what it will finally be like.

David's table was designed for a young child to stand beside to use as a play surface. How do you suppose he calculated the dimensions of the table? Why do you suppose he rounded the four corners? The underframe was made from round-sectioned material which was stained bright red. How might the legs be drilled to receive the round-sectioned rails accurately?

Joely designed her table as a plant stand. She wanted the construction to appear very slender. Why do you suppose she chose metal for this design?

## Tables for drawing

Very often we need a working surface of a much more specialised nature. Drawing tables are a good example of this. In some situations they can be used almost like ordinary tables, but they may also need to convert into a precision instrument. Sometimes the precision drawing unit can be clipped onto an existing table, but in other situations it is useful to have a complete drawing table.

Russell designed a table-top drawing unit. He particularly wanted the unit to fold away flat and yet be able to fix at a variety of working angles. He also designed a method of producing a parallel-motion

device. It was a modification of the traditional tee-square design, with the stock running in a channel of aluminium alloy. Think about what design methods he used to produce a satisfactory solution to his problem.

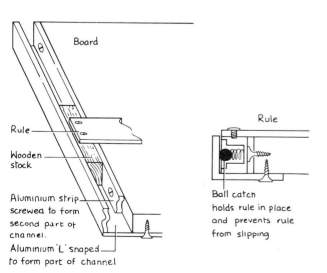

Board
Rule
Wooden stock
Aluminium strip screwed to form second part of channel.
Aluminium 'L' shaped to form part of channel

Rule
Ball catch holds rule in place and prevents rule from slipping

65

## Tables for drawing (continued)

Special working tables have to be particularly cleverly designed if they are to combine a range of functions. It gets even more difficult if the unit has only a very limited space to fit into.

Jayne's unit was designed in such a way that it would locate in a relatively confined area in her small bedroom. The unit was mounted on castors so that when it was needed it could be wheeled out. The left-hand side of the unit could be pulled out to offer a working surface. The drawers contained drawing instruments and paper. This unit obviously incorporates a range of functions.

The ergonomics of 'dual function' units can get very critical, and it becomes more and more important to prepare detailed working drawings of how the unit appears, what it should be made of and how it will be constructed.

The structure of Jayne's unit was designed around the use of a 'Dexion Speedframe'. The lengths of tubing were cut and then forced onto the special castings which made up the corner joints and 'tee' joints. Before she started to cut any material, however, Jayne drew out an **exploded drawing** of the structure, showing which joint-pieces she needed, how many and how they were going to make up into the whole structure. This drawing was very helpful in making sure she ordered the right number of units, and the right length of tubing.

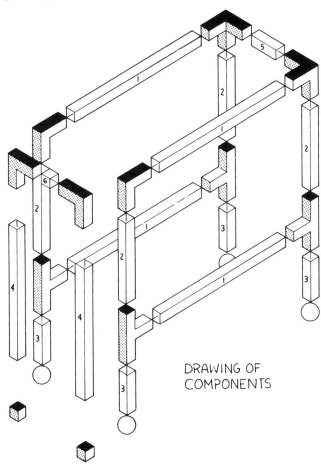

DRAWING OF COMPONENTS

| PART | No | LENGTH | TUBOTEX | | DEXION |
|---|---|---|---|---|---|
| ① LENGTH | 4 OFF | 1000 mm | £ 17·96 | | |
| ② UPRIGHT | 4 OFF | 500 mm | £ 11·96 | | |
| ③ UPRIGHT | 4 OFF | 250 mm | £ 5·16 | 4 x 12' Lengths £ 29 | |
| ④ LEGS | 2 OFF | 800 mm | £ 6·98 | | |
| ⑤ CROSSPIECE | 1 OFF | 600 mm | £ 2·99 | | |
| ⑥ CROSSPIECE | 1 OFF | 560 mm | £ 2·99 | | |
| | | | | | |
| 2 CORNERS | | | £ 3·58 | | £ 3·23 |
| 4 TEE JOINS | | | £ 7·96 | | £ 7·80 |
| 2 90° JOINS | | | £ 3·98 | | £ 7·80 |
| 2 END CAPS | | | £ ·28 | | £ ·24 |
| 4 50mm CASTORS | | | £ 0·76 | | £ 9·35 |
| | | TOTAL | £ 70·60 | | £ 57·42 |

▲ Alternative costing

Study this part of a working drawing carefully. You will see it shows an electric kettle. This is the sort of detail that you should aim to get into your final drawings before you start to make anything. A good rule to follow is that you ought to be able to send your drawing through the post to a manufacturer who must be able to understand exactly what needs to be made. Some points to think about when designing any product are:

- materials should be specified
- all sizes should be dimensioned
- jointing techniques should be labelled
- finishes should be noted
- bought-in components should be specified.

Now look at the drawing again, and see if you could make the product with *only* the information from this drawing.

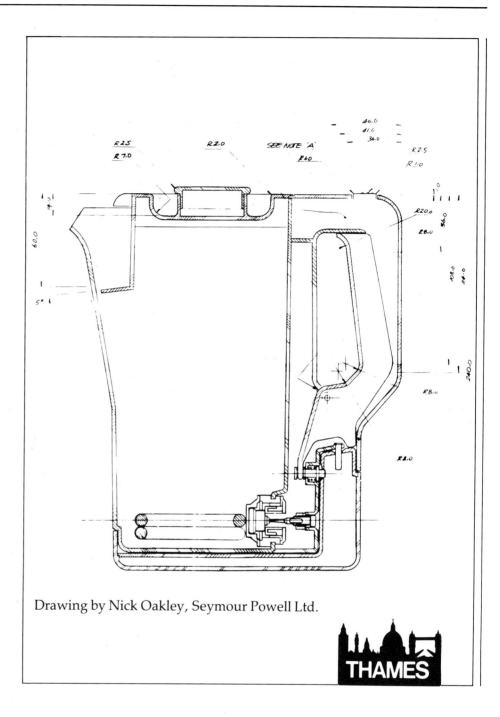

Drawing by Nick Oakley, Seymour Powell Ltd.

## Activities

1. Design and make a working surface for a young child which incorporates a seat. The product should help the child in creative play by being adaptable for different uses. It could, perhaps, become a boat or a dog kennel.

2. Produce some designs for a small table which is to be made up from three interlocking geometrical shapes cut from a piece of 12 mm thick acrylic sheet measuring 900 mm × 450 mm.

3. Make up a chart of a number of surfaces in your home. What are they made from and how have they

been finished? Why do you think each material has been used the way it has and could the surfaces be improved upon with other materials?

4. Can you picture a confined area in your own home into which a work station could be fitted? Think about the range of functions you would like it to perform. How would you approach the design of it?

5. What are the advantages of using a non-permanent fixing, such as 'Dexion Speedframe', for the structure of a cabinet or drawing table? What are the problems?

Many of you will have younger brothers and sisters or will have friends who do. Observing young children at play is a very important starting point for thinking about the design of children's toys.

There is an almost infinite variety of toys for young children to play with. But think about and observe them and then write down the features of a *good* toy. Which of the following things should toys do for children. Think of a particular age range (e.g. 0–1 yrs or 5–8 yrs) and decide whether they should:

● entertain
● occupy
● fascinate
● comfort
● challenge
● teach.

Or should all toys do all of these things for all ages of children? Talk to the parents of a toddler whom you know, and ask them to tell you what their child's favourite toy is. Study the toy carefully, and how the child plays with it, and then write down the qualities in it that seem to appeal to the child.

## *Moving toys*

This project began with the pupils investigating **movement** as the basic ingredient of a toy. The movement might be direct – like a child pushing or pulling it along. Or it could be indirect, where one movement or action creates a different movement somewhere else – like a pull-along duck that shakes its head or waddles its feet.

### Syringes and tubing

This system of movement works by a fluid being pushed between two syringes which act as pistons inside cylinders. By pressing one end of the system (usually called the **master cylinder**), the fluid is forced along the tubing and it pushes the other end out (usually called the **slave cylinder**).

### Balloons and 'squeezies'

This system works by air moving between two flexible containers – usually a balloon at one end and a 'squeezy' bottle at the other. When the air is squeezed out of the bottle it inflates a balloon. This then drives the moving part of the toy.

### Using syringes

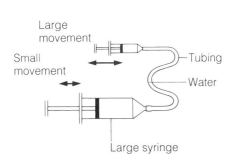
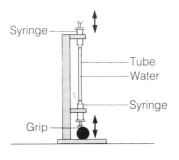
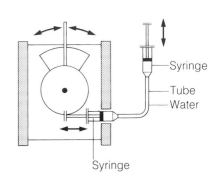

### Using balloons

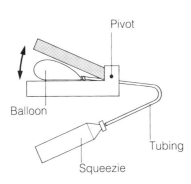
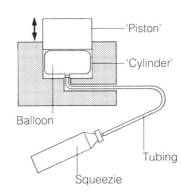
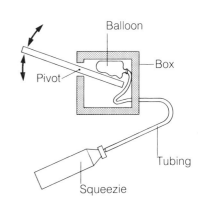

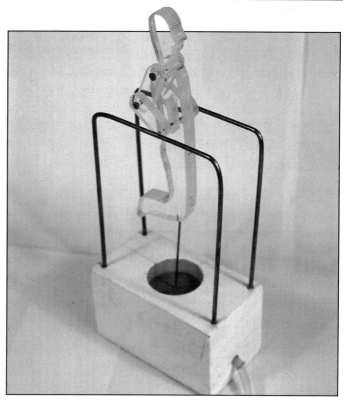

David decided to design and make a fork-lift truck which worked by the syringe principle. Gary used the same principle to make an acrobat. If you had to design toys of this sort, how would you sort out the details of the movement? What sort of modelling would you have to do?

Joely decided to use the squeezy system. Her train makes use of the length of tubing as the 'cord' of her pull-along toy. As the train 'puffs' along the smoke billows up out of the funnel. What would you have made the smoke from? How would you have made it?

## Activities

1. Using a simple system like the ones on this page, design a toy which can be made to move across a carpeted surface through the operation of the system alone. No pulling or pushing is allowed.

2. Design a toy that will produce a jerky or uneven movement as it is pulled along a surface.

3. Make a list of the different types of toys which the young children you have seen play with. Sort them out into categories such as dynamic, static, decorative, functional, educational and so on.

4. Write to a major toy manufacturer for a catalogue. Study the types of toys that are recommended for particular age groups. What are the major features that determine the age suitability of a toy?

Other examples of moving toys can be seen here. The spaghetti-man toy has only been put together after an enormous amount of experimenting with mechanical movements. All the materials are very simple, but they are very cleverly assembled.

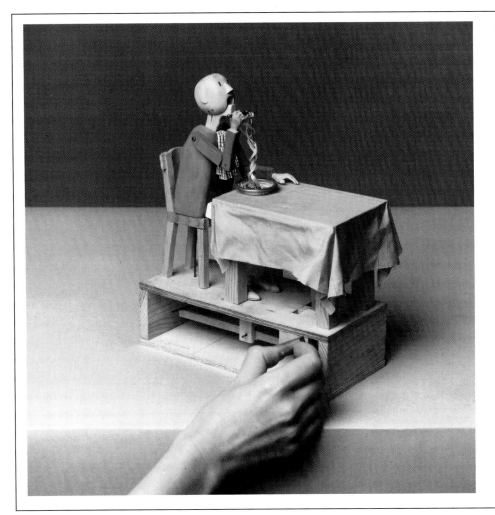

6 *My engineering is not so serious that you need exactly the same result every time. I like making things that don't take too long, I like to use materials that don't cost an awful lot and I like to get a bit of fun out of things.* 9

Paul Spooner

THAMES

These toys resulted from a project in which a group of pupils was asked to incorporate a simple rotary crank action into a child's toy.

### Interlocking toys and puzzles

These pupils observed and recorded young children playing with interlocking toys like Lego. They were able to see the importance of safety, colour, size and simplicity of use. When they began to detail their own proposals they came across the major problem. Each of their ideas required the production of numbers of components – and many of them had to be *identical* if the toy was to work properly.

Lisa decided to produce an 'H'-shaped brick which would stack together in a number of different ways. She chose a casting operation to produce the identical units in a mould made from a flexible vinyl moulding material.

Lee made his units from acrylic sheet, whilst John's units were produced from solid wooden blocks. This made it possible to prepare lengths of the wood from which the individual pieces could be cut. This helped with the accuracy, but he found that even applying a finish to the timber made a 'good' fit into a 'too tight' one.

Graham's 'molecular' structure succeeded mainly because of the jig he made to hold each block in exactly the same position for drilling.

## Activities

1. Collect a range of Lego bricks and measure their dimensions with as accurate a tool as you can. A micrometer would be ideal. Record the variation in critical sizes from brick to brick. You will be amazed at how accurate they are. Plot the information on a graph or block chart.

2. Consider the problems of producing a large number of identically-sized units. Assume you want to cut 75 mm circles, and are going to cut them from 6 mm plywood. How many ways can you think of to do it?

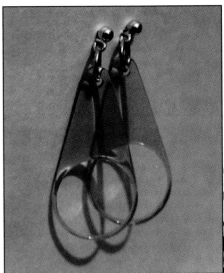

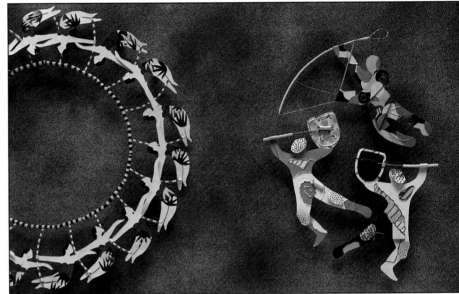

The ever-increasing range of exciting and colourful materials allows the designer to experiment and develop quite new approaches to body adornment. Even when the basic items of adornment are the ordinary conventional ones, such as . . .

- rings
- ear-rings
- pendants
- necklaces
- bracelets
- hair pins/clips/slides
- glasses . . .

it is still possible to develop unusual, interesting and exciting products.

Look at the range of items on these pages and think about the materials and production techniques that have been used to achieve the special effects.

Laminating thin materials together can create a wide range of effects. Here you can see laminated wood veneers and laminated acrylic sheet.

You can buy brightly-coloured plastic-coated wire from engineering modellers' suppliers. But think about how you can achieve the different sorts of bending and joining that can go into this sort of product.

Repeated forms are often used in the design of necklaces and bracelets. The main problems here concern the means of joining the segments together so that the whole unit can be flexible.

Several of these pieces were produced by 4th and 5th form pupils in schools. Can you tell them from the professional ones? And can you see how you could make products of similar quality?

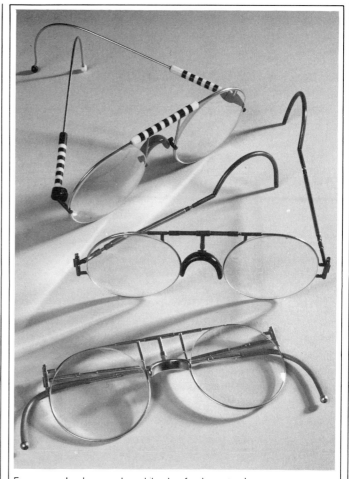

Even spectacles can be objects of adornment

## Activities

1. Look carefully at a number of different ways of fastening a belt. Find out where you can buy leather or suitable belt fabrics. Design for yourself a belt buckle and belt which will hold up a pair of jeans or trousers.
2. Design and make a badge that shows your membership of a club or society. Would you have to co-ordinate this with any specialist clothing?
3. Signet rings were traditionally used as letter stamps in the days when sealing wax was used to seal letters. Can you design an item of body adornment that also has a specific function? What about glasses for reading in the dark?

A common characteristic of the human race is the desire to make music. This may be done with nothing more than the voice, but often involves the use of specific musical instruments. Some of these can be very sophisticated and others very simple. You may be interested in making music yourself, and the design of new musical instruments can be fascinating.

## What makes music?

The basic principles of musical instruments are all dependent on vibrating the air, and methods of forcing the air to vibrate include:

- plucking strings
- blowing pipes
- hitting skins or other surfaces.

All these methods are used in traditional devices to make the air around the instrument vibrate, and it is this vibration that we hear.

Traditional instrument making is a highly-skilled craft that is usually very personal and labour intensive. The products tend to be intricate and often highly ornamented, with the result that they are also very expensive.

Simply reproducing existing traditional instruments does not offer much design opportunity, but with a bit of imagination you can begin to modify and redesign instruments of your own.

A string can be made to vibrate by plucking it or rubbing something across it. The length, thickness and means of vibrating the string alter the note.

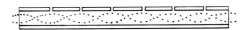

The air inside a tube can be made to vibrate with a whistle, a reed, vibrating lips or blowing across it. Alter the length of tube to alter the note.

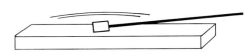

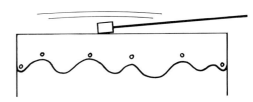

Skins and solid objects can be hit to make them vibrate. The size and density of the solid objects alter the note, the size and tautness of the skin alters the sound.

Christopher experimented with a range of skin-like materials to design a set of 'tom-tom' drums. He found that he could vary the sound considerably by changing the size of the container and the tautness of the skin, as well as the material that it was made from. He eventually made a hollow octagonal structure out of alternating pieces of oak and mahogany.

Tom-toms

Julie designed a set of chime-bars on a stand for her little brother's nursery school. Apart from the problems of getting the right material for the bars, she found that the hanging system was very important to the quality of the sound. Having found a way of getting the right technical effects, she then had to consider all the ergonomic and design factors that go into a child's musical toy.

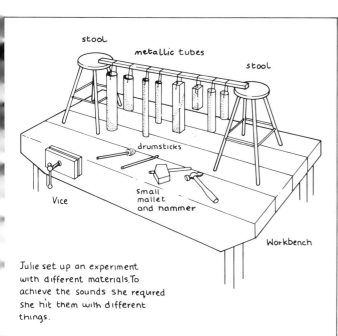

Julie set up an experiment with different materials. To achieve the sounds she required she hit them with different things.

Many musical instruments rely on the use of more recent technologies for the production of sounds. Nick designed and built a 'syn-drum'. He did not have enough time to design his own electronic circuitry, so he researched what was available commercially. The rest of the design, however, was completely original, and a wide range of special effects can be created by connecting the syn-drum with a microcomputer.

Syndrum

Electronic drum machine

## Activities

1. Design and make a carrying case for a small electronic keyboard. The case should open out in such a way that it can be used as a support, stand and console for the instrument.

2. Research the sound qualities of the materials which you find in your school workshop. Use the results of your research to design a xylophone suitable for batch production for a local primary school.

3. Design and make a holder which can be used for an electric or an acoustic guitar. It should be able to support either instrument and be very stable.

4. What ergonomic and design factors should Julie have taken into account for her chime-bar project for the nursery school?

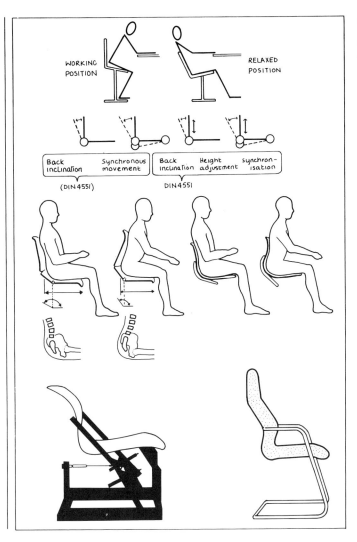

One of the most complex pieces of furniture to design and make is a chair or seating unit. There are so many things to bear in mind in its design, particularly:

- specific functional considerations
- structural considerations
- ergonomic considerations
- aesthetic considerations, bearing in mind the environment in which it will be used.

With all these variations, it is hardly surprising that there is a huge range of chairs available.

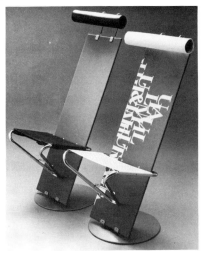

In order to get the ergonomics of her chair right, Anna made an 'ergonome' (a scale model of a person) which she was able to bend into a number of different positions. By using this, she was able to try out the card models of chair designs with her card person.

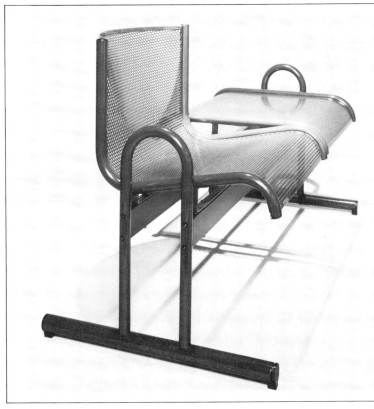

❝ The multiple-unit Transit chair was originally designed for the British Airport Authority, whose main priority was that it must be fire resistant and hence made of metal. The Authority was really worried that metal couldn't produce a comfortable seat. ❞

Rodney Kinsman

She wanted a relaxing chair in her bedroom, and she liked the idea of making a tubular steel frame with a canvas seat. Anna explored the possibilities of using plumbing fittings in the structure that enabled her to screw it together. What other techniques could she have used to create the same visual effect? What are the advantages of the system she used?

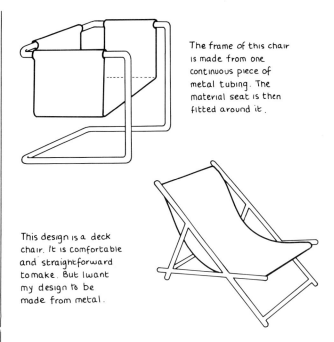

The frame of this chair is made from one continuous piece of metal tubing. The material seat is then fitted around it.

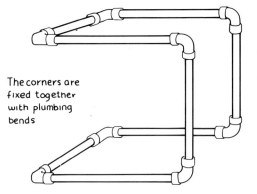

The corners are fixed together with plumbing bends

Tubular steel lengths of 600mm The lengths are hollow and 38mm across

This design is a deck chair. It is comfortable and straightforward to make. But I want my design to be made from metal.

Peter wanted an upright working chair for use with his drawing unit. The final height position was very important, so he built a simple adjustment into the central column. How would you do this?

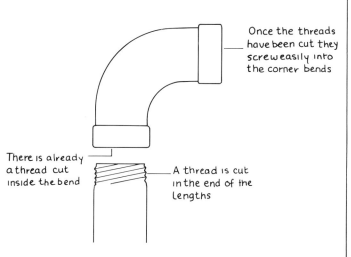

Once the threads have been cut they screw easily into the corner bends

There is already a thread cut inside the bend

A thread is cut in the end of the lengths

## Activities

1. Find out about some seating units that are made for very specialised purposes (such as for handicapped people or racing drivers). What are the major differences between these sorts of seating and ordinary domestic seating?

2. Produce a design for a test rig to find the most favourable seating position for the widest possible range of functions.

3. What changes have been brought about in furniture design by the growth of 'knock down' self-assembly furniture? When designing such a piece of furniture what additional restrictions does the designer have to cope with?

4. Make a study of seat-covering materials that includes:
   - the durability of the material
   - the techniques that can be used to join and fix it
   - the structure of the material
   - the legal and safety considerations (for instance, in the case of fire)
   - the potential for decorative treatment
   - the cost of the material.

# Realisation Checklist

This checklist shows the content of your Design and Realisation course in a simple form.

## Common Core

i) The elements of designing, making and evaluating as outlined in the common core section of the book, including:

- problems and needs
- statement of a brief
- research and analysis
- generating and developing ideas
- realising ideas
- evaluating ideas and realisations
- communicating with words and visual images model making.

ii) Design in society, which you should think about under the two headings of **being a designer** and **being a user**. Some of the following issues may feature in your course:

- product design as part of a designed environment
- dependence on energy – past, present and future
- aesthetics of industrially-produced items
- mass production
- automation and robotics
- consumer awareness
- conservation
- pollution
- ecology
- design for minority groups.

There are two particular areas which require careful study. They are ergonomics and the technological principles and concepts upon which design and realisation work is based.

## Ergonomics

- Human dimensions and physical attributes.
- Production of an ergonome.
- Feasibility testing with mock-ups and so on.

## Technological principles and concepts

- Forces and structures (a qualitative understanding only) using common examples. No calculations required.

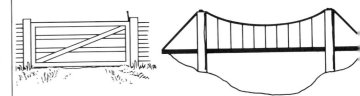

- Compression, tension, torsion, leverage, shear, bending moments, equilibrium, stability, distortion and stiffness. Holding and locking, jigs, cramps and so on.

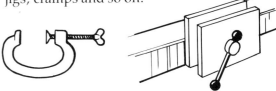

- Energy – wind, water, solar, geothermal, gas, oil, coal, nuclear, electrical storage, electrical conversion and the control, release and uses of energy.

- Movement and mechanics – levers, links, gears, racks, pulleys, cams, bearings, belts, chains, sprockets, rotational and linear adjustment.

- Electrical – earthing, insulation, conduction, resistance, fusing, switching.

The next two parts of this checklist concern the elements which are of great importance to the realisation stages of your work. They are the **materials** which you are most likely to use and the **processes of manufacture**. It is hoped that most knowledge of this nature is gained through actual practical experience. However, you are unlikely to work with all of these processes or use every material. This is not necessarily a problem, as you will find that your experiences with one material or process can, with common sense, be transferred to other processes and problems.

## *Materials*
### Basic categories
- wood, metal- and plastic-resilient materials
- ceramics, textiles and concrete

### Availability of materials
- commonly available stock sizes
- form of supply

### Costing of materials

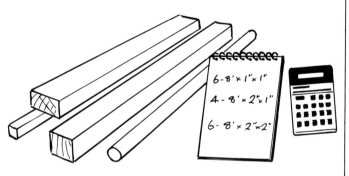

### Testing of materials
### Properties of materials
- hardness (hardening and tempering of steel), density
- malleability (annealing), ductility
- strength, durability
- conductivity, insulative properties
- working properties likely to be encountered in the school

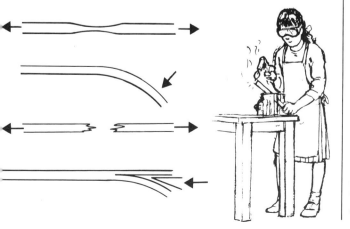

### Choosing materials
- concept of suitability and situation for use
- comparability of different materials

### Woods
Common hardwoods
Common softwoods
Plywood
Blockboard
Chipboard
Hardboard

### Metals
Iron – cast and wrought
Black and BDM steel
Cast and tool steels
Copper, zinc, tin, lead, aluminium and alloys, such as bronze and brass

### Plastics
Thermosetting
Thermoplastic
Acrylic, PVC
GRP, PTFE
Nylon, ABS
Polythene powder

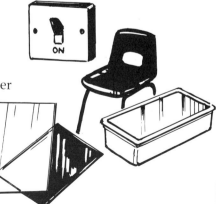

There are a number of extra materials that you can use, such as paint, bolts and emery paper. These are usually referred to as **ancillary** materials. They are mentioned in the next section.

## *Elements of manufacture*

Manufacture may include one or all of the following.

### Preparation

- marking out, parallels, 90 and 45 degree angles
- measurement, checking
- datums, centre lines

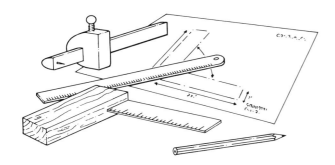

### Assembly of a number of components

- joints (the fashioning of interlocking parts)
- welding, brazing, soldering
- nails, screws
- pop rivets, rivets, nuts and bolts
- knock-down fittings, hinges and handles
- adhesives for similar and dissimilar materials

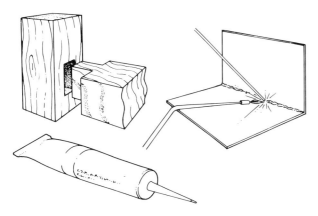

### Deforming a material from its usual state

- laminating timber
- forging metal, hollowing (and planishing)
- bending and forming acrylic (and plastic memory)
- vacuum forming

### Removal of unwanted material

- hand and machine processes

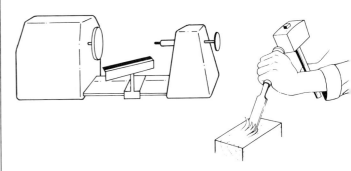

### Casting a material in a liquid state into a mould

- aluminium alloy, resin, concrete

### Finishing

- surface quality, performance and aesthetics, colour
- corrosion, damage, wear, lubrication and protection
- abrasives, papers, grits, wools, pads, grades
- penetrative finishes such as creosote, sealers, case hardening
- surface-layer finishes such as paint, varnish, plastic coating, galvanising

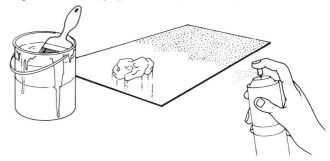

### Hand and machine tools

- emphasis on correct use through coursework, knowledge of correct name and principle of operation
- dividing materials – saws, shears and knives
- trimming materials – files, planes, chisels, spokeshaves
- hitting – hammers and mallets
- making holes – drills, bits, plug cutter, hole saw
- buffing machine
- lathe, milling machine, shaping machine, wood lathe, sanding disc

# Examination Checklist

This table gives you a general guide to the different patterns of coursework and examination papers required by each of the five GCSE Examining Groups. You should ask your teacher for the precise details of the course which you are following. The following points would be useful to know:

- the type and number of questions
- the choice of questions
- how the questions are presented
- how the answers are to be presented
- what the assessment form looks like, and what it expects you to produce.

| | % | Term 1 | Term 2 | Term 3 | Term 4 | Term 5 | Term 6 Examination |
|---|---|---|---|---|---|---|---|
| **LONDON AND EAST ANGLIAN GROUP** | | | | | | | |
| Coursework   Design/Making | 20/20 | ← | | | | → | |
| Paper 1   Design and Realisation project | 30 | | | | | ← | → 5 hrs |
| Paper 2   Syllabus knowledge | 30 | | | | | | 2 hrs |
| **MIDLAND EXAMINING GROUP** | | | | | | | |
| Coursework   Design Realisation | 15/15 | ← | | | | → | |
| Paper 1   Written Paper | 30 | | | | | | 2¼ hrs |
| Paper 2   Design | 20 | | | | | ←→ | |
| Paper 3   Design Realisation | 20 | | | | | | Up to 20 hrs |
| **NORTHERN EXAMINING ASSOCIATION** | | | | | | | |
| Coursework project   Design Communication/Manufacture | 15/35 | | | ← | | → | |
| Paper 1   Design Research/Communication | 30 | | | | | ← | → 1¾ hrs |
| Paper 2   Syllabus knowledge | 20 | | | | | | 1¾ hrs |
| **SOUTHERN EXAMINING GROUP** | | | | | | | |
| Coursework   Design and Realisation | 20/30 | ← | | | | → | |
| Paper 1   Materials/Tools/Processes/Technology | 25 | | | | | | 2 hrs |
| Paper 2   Research and Written | 25 | | | | | ←→ | 2 hrs |
| **WELSH JOINT EDUCATION COMMITTEE** | | | | | | | |
| Design Study | 50 | | | ← | | → | |
| Paper 1   Design | 20 | | | | | | 3 hrs |
| Paper 2   Technology and Design Thinking | 30 | | | | | | 2 hrs |

The CDT Technology course is designed to open your eyes to the enormous contribution that technology makes to people's lives and their work. In addition, the course is designed to give you more competence and confidence in tackling technological problems for yourself.

Technology does not exist for itself, but as a servant for all of us – intended to make our lives safer, easier and generally more pleasurable. From the humblest of products (like a paper-clip) to the most sophisticated products and systems (like the space shuttle), their design, development and manufacture have involved some common principles that you will be introduced to in this course.

### What's in a paper-clip?

Its design may be very simple – but even in that you would have to think about its **function** and **use**. Two questions to think about are:

- How big does it need to be?
- What form and colour should it have?

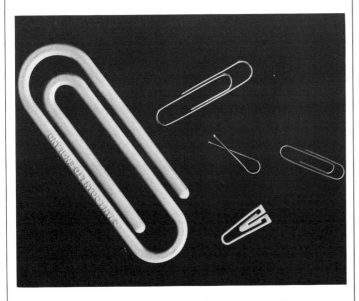

But the really important thing about paper-clips is that they must be cheap and plentiful. And as a designer and technologist this takes you into the worlds of mass manufacturing, automation, packaging, distribution, advertising and retailing.

### How do you choose the right material?

It has to be strong enough and springy enough to hold its shape after repeated flexing.

It must be able to be mass-produced quickly, and in this case that means in a multi-part die for injection moulding.

The plastic material from which the clip is to be made has to be manufactured from raw materials – probably crude oil – which themselves have to be obtained and refined.

The temperature of the injected plastic (and the temperature of the mould it is being injected into) have to be carefully controlled to ensure consistency. This involves sophisticated temperature sensors and an electronic read-out system.

The plastic has to be injected at very high pressure to ensure a good-quality product. This involves high pressure hydraulic engineering – both for the injection mechanism and for the clamps that close and open the mould.

When the paper-clip comes from the injection moulder it moves down a conveyor belt to be sorted and automatically batched for packing. Light sensors can be used to count the paper-clips, and a simple mechanical system sorts them into 10s, 50s, 100s or whatever number is pre-selected for the package.

The package itself – usually a cardboard box – has to be stamped from flat sheet, folded up and fixed into the box form before the paper-clips can be loaded into it.

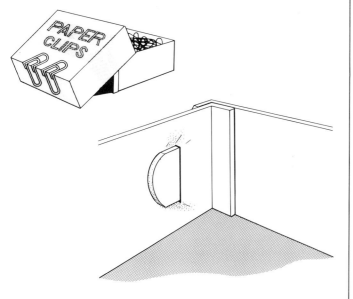

The loading might be done by hand, or it might be mechanised as part of the batching process, or it might even be automated with some type of robotic packing system. Similarly, the boxes will be packed into cartons for distribution.

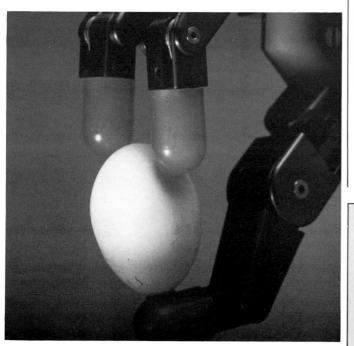

Precision handling by robot

The warehouse that stores the cartons may have a human system for loading and stacking or an automated system with robotic fork-lift trucks following pre-selected programmes.

Automated selection of computer tapes

When you buy one of the boxes from the shop, the till operator is increasingly likely to have a 'bar-code' light-sensing pen that will automatically read the product, charge the latest price and at the same time alert the warehouse to replace the sold item.

### Now what's in a paper-clip?
It is impossible to look at any product, however simple, without seeing the results of countless technological developments.

## Activities

1. Research the 'life cycle' of another simple product, showing the impact of various technologies on its development.

2. Think about how the contribution of human workers has been reduced by the developments in technology. How has this development grown in the last 5, 10, 20, 50 years?

When you design anything, one of the most important decisions you will have to make is which materials to use. It is important to choose wisely because you will want your design to work well, look good and last a long time. The materials you choose will govern whether this is the case or not.

Look at the photograph of the desk below. Each of the parts is made from a different material. Below are given some of the reasons why the designer chose the materials that he did.

Artist's impression

3D model

Designed by
Paul Stead

i) **Medium density fibreboard** (mdf) is used for the desk top. It is easily obtained in large, flat sheets. It has good machining properties (unlike chipboard), so the edge could be made curved. When stained and lacquered this curved edge looks attractive and can take quite hard knocks.

ii) **Linoleum** (lino) is used to cover the desk top. It feels comfortable to work on and provides a softer surface than the mdf. Ball-point pens don't 'skid' off the paper. It is hard-wearing, easy to attach to the mdf and can be obtained in a wide range of colours.

iii) The legs of the desk are made from wide **steel tubes**. Steel is both stiff and strong. It is not very scratch resistant and rusts, so it has been protected by **hammerite** – an enamel paint that is sprayed onto the steel and then baked hard in an oven. The hammerite prevents the legs from getting chipped or scratched and stops them rusting.

iv) The curved sliding door is made from interlinking tubes of **ABS plastic**. ABS is strong and stiff enough to make a firm door but not so stiff as to stop the tubes 'snapping' together into place.

The designer of the desk knew a lot about what these materials were like – their **properties** – and how they could be shaped – their **working characteristics**. He also knew a lot about the properties and working characteristics of other materials in order to reject them in favour of those chosen. Panel 1 summarises some of the important properties that designers use to describe what materials are like. Panel 2 summarises the properties and working characteristics of metals, plastics and timber products. Use these panels in tackling the activities.

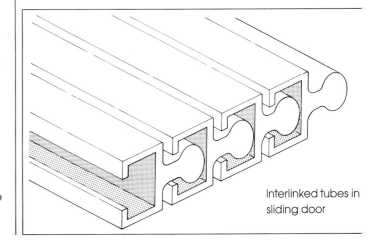

Interlinked tubes in
sliding door

## Panel 1 – The important properties of materials

**Strength** – this tells us how easy or difficult it is to break the material.

**Toughness** – this tells us how much impact the material can withstand without breaking.

**Hardness** – this tells us how scratch resistant a material is.

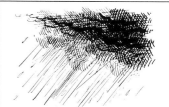

**Resistance to the environment** – this tells us how easily a material rots or corrodes.

**Density** – this tells us how heavy a material is compared to its size. Materials with a low density are light for their size, and can float. High density materials sink.

**Stiffness** – this tells us how easy it is to stretch or squash a material. Very stiff materials are difficult to stretch or squash.

**Thermal conductivity** – this tells us how warm or cold the material will feel when we touch it. High conductivity materials feel cold and are poor insulators. Low conductivity materials feel warm and are good insulators.

## Panel 2 – Characteristics of materials

**Metals**

High density, high stiffness, high strength, high toughness, moderately hard, high conductivity, likely to corrode.

Sheet metals are more difficult to shape and form than thermoplastics.
Easily machined.

**Timber products**

Low density, moderate stiffness, moderate strength, low toughness, low hardness, low conductivity, rot easily.

Timber sheets are difficult to shape and form.

Machining characteristics vary considerably.

**Plastics**

Low density, low stiffness, low strength, low toughness, low hardness, low conductivity, high resistance to corrosion and rotting.

Thermosetting plastics are usually stiffer, stronger and harder than thermoplastics but do not soften reversibly on heating.

Thermoplastic sheet is easily shaped and formed using heat and pressure.

Machining characteristics are similar to metals.

## Activities

1. Try to work out what it would be like using the desk shown in the photographs on page 84 if:
   a) the desk top was made of painted steel;
   b) the legs were made of ABS plastic;
   c) the sliding door was made from strips of mdf.

2. Collect some plastic cutlery and some metal cutlery. Compare their design and performance and explain the differences in terms of the properties of metal and plastic.

3. The diagram opposite shows a kite. What properties will the materials used for the parts which are labelled need to have? Which materials would you use for these parts?

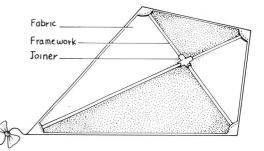

Fabric
Framework
Joiner

Whenever there are moving parts in something there is a **mechanism**. Mechanisms are designed to achieve any movements that are required. Look at the hand whisk opposite. Try to work out what movements take place. Firstly, there has to be an input movement. This is provided by a human hand. Your hand will move in a circle as it turns the handle. This input is described as **rotary**. The output in response to this input is the motion of the whisks. How will this differ from the input? Is it still rotary? Is it at the same speed or has it got faster or slower? If it is rotary, is it in the same plane? The diagram next to the photo of the whisk will help you answer these questions.

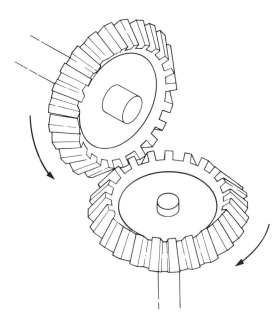

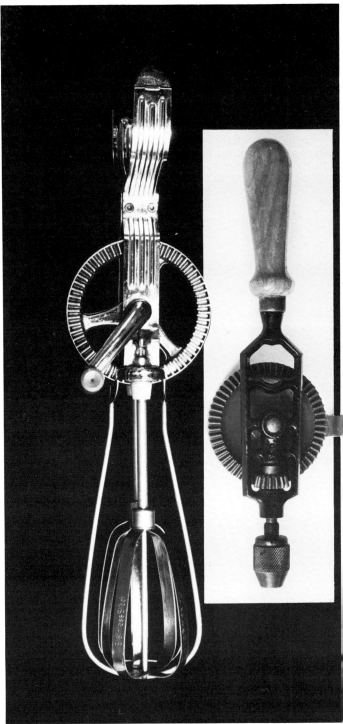

The difference between input and output motions is caused by a large gear wheel with lots of teeth moving a small gear wheel with few teeth mounted at right angles to it. The figure opposite shows a hand drill. You should be able to see that the input and output movements are similar to those in the whisk. Look carefully at the photographs and work out what is different in the two mechanisms.

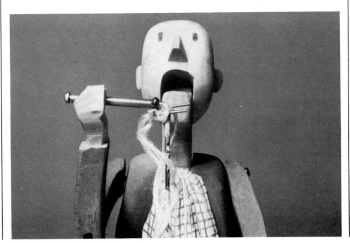

When you design a mechanism it is important that you know the input movement and output movement you require. You will need to think the problem through from both ends. In the spaghetti-eating man shown on page 70, the designer knew that he wanted the mouth to open and close – an up-and-down movement of the skull. This is the output. He wanted the input to be a rotary movement, provided by someone turning a handle.

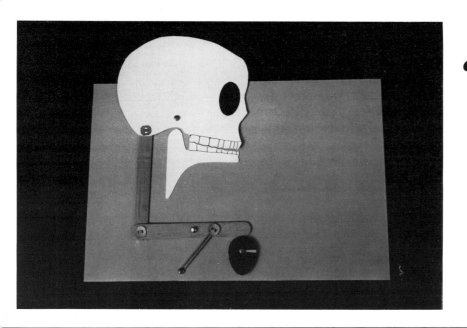

> *It's much better to think about the mechanism using easy-to-work materials, like cardboard and lolly-pop sticks, which you can shape easily and then get a mechanism which works from that, before you go on to make it in a much more difficult material.*
>
> Dave Barlex

The details of a mechanism used to do this are shown above. When the cam revolves the egg shape pushes one end of the lever A upwards. The other end of this lever moves down and the linkage between it and the skull pulls the base of the skull down. As the skull is pivoted on the jaw bone, the mouth opens. Try to write down how the cam causes the mouth to close and stay shut.

The toy snail shown here moves along the floor in a straight line with its head moving in and out of its shell. There are many ways to achieve this movement. The figure below shows the internal workings at various stages in the movement. The input is provided by a clockwork motor. This drives the large wheel (A). The peg (B) on this wheel moves up and down in the slot (C) and pushes the head backward and forward. Stationary pegs on the shell fit into the slot (D) and guide this movement.

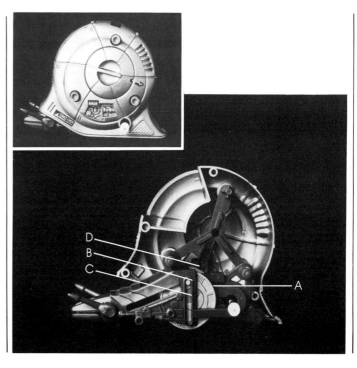

## Activities

1. Make a neat line-diagram tracing of the mouth-opening mechanism of the spaghetti man. Redraw this diagram with the cam rotated 90°, 180° and 270° from the original position. Show the positions of the lever, linkage and skull in each case.

   What changes would you make if:
   a) You wanted the mouth to open and close *twice* for every revolution of the cam?
   b) You wanted the mouth to chew?
   c) You wanted the mouth to *snap* shut?
   d) You wanted the mouth to open wider, like in a long yawn?
   e) You wanted the mouth to 'talk' very fast?

2. Make a simple model of the head-controlling mechanism in the snail toy. Use stiff card, paper fasteners and 'lolly' sticks. What alterations can you make to the mechanism to give a more interesting movement – fast out and slow in, for example?

# Structures

## What are structures?

Structures are around us all the time in both the natural and the made world. Several are shown on this page. Any structure has to be able to support its own weight and resist any additional forces it meets, otherwise it will collapse. So a working definition of a structure is anything that supports a load. In addition it may be responsible for enclosing a particular space and protecting whatever is in that space.

Look at the structures on this page and identify:
- the loads they support
- any space they enclose
- whatever they protect.

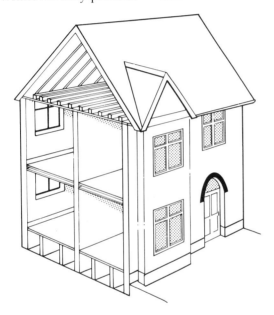

### Stability and balance

It is important that a structure is stable. When in use it should not tip over. What might happen to the tower crane if the large weight were missing? What would happen to the sea urchin if its lower legs came down to a point beneath its body rather than spread out?

▲ Hong Kong and Shanghai bank in Hong Kong

▲ Modelling structures with lolly sticks and paper fasteners

## Activity 1

Using card, make silhouette models of objects in which balance is important. Investigate their stability by seeing how far you can lean them over before they topple. Objects you might model are those pictured, or chairs, stools, double-decker buses, people in various positions, table lamps or wine glasses. Work out ways of improving the stability of your model. This may involve changing the shape in some way, keeping the shape the same and adding extra weight somewhere, or a mixture of both. Compare your model and improvements with the performance and structure of the actual items.

## Forces in structures

When a load is placed on a structure, parts of the structure will react against the loading. Parts that are stretched by the loading are said to be in **tension**. Parts that are squashed by the load are in **compression**. You can often tell which parts of a framework are in tension or compression by building models from thin stick and string. To begin with build the model using just sticks joined together with paper fasteners, as shown on the opposite page. You can check whether a part is in tension or compression by replacing it with string. String gets tighter under tension but collapses under compression.

## Deflection and failure

When a structure is loaded, parts of it will **deflect**. Parts that are under tension will get longer, parts that are under compression will get shorter. It is important that these deflections are temporary, so that when the loading is removed the parts return to their original shape and length.

Designers go to great lengths to avoid structural failure, although they have to allow for deflection. With large structures used by lots of people (like bridges or skyscrapers), the result of failure can be a major disaster. So each part of a structure is designed to be several times stronger than it needs to be under normal loading conditions. This is called using safety factors. Look back to the Materials section and find out which materials are stiff (have small deflections) and strong. What are these materials used for?

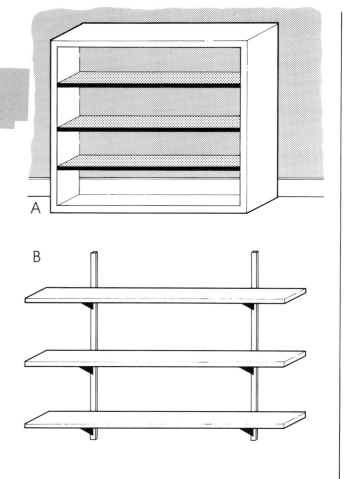

A

B

## Activity 2

Build stick models of a roof truss or tower crane. For a particular loading try to predict which parts are in tension and which in compression. Check your prediction using string. Alter the loading position and see if this causes any changes.

## Activity 3

The diagram above shows two sets of book shelves – A and B. A is free-standing, and the shelves are beams supported at each end by the uprights. B is fixed to a wall, and the shelves are beams supported by cantilever spur units some distance from the end of each shelf. Using card and thin stick build simple models of A and B. Use the models to answer these questions:

i) Where and in what direction does deflection take place when the shelf is loaded with books?
ii) How is this deflection affected by the length, breadth and depth of the shelf?
iii) Which parts of the loaded structure are in tension, and which are in compression?

iv) What balance problems might there be if shelves are loaded unevenly?

If you want to make a real set of book shelves you will need to investigate the following:
i) What sizes are books? Which dimensions are important for shelf design?
ii) How much does a 'shelf's worth' of books weigh?
iii) What deflections occur with this loading on shelves of different material?
iv) What deflections are acceptable?

Whenever you do work of any kind you use energy. The main source of energy is the Sun. Sunlight provides the energy for plants and trees to produce their foodstuffs from carbon dioxide and water in the atmosphere. Fossil fuels – like coal and oil – act like the Earth's energy store, and when we burn them we release the energy of ancient sunlight trapped many millions of years ago.

The energy in fossil fuels can be used to drive machines directly (for instance, in motor vehicles), but most of it is used to create heat and to generate electricity. However, the use of fossil fuels in this way does have some drawbacks, as it is thought by many people to create environmental problems such as acid rain. Nuclear fuel – which some people believe can provide an almost unlimited amount of clean energy – can be used to generate electricity. However, its use has similarly been surrounded by controversy, especially since the disaster at the nuclear reactor at Chernobyl in 1986.

By whatever means it is created, electricity is the most incredibly useful and versatile form of energy. Unfortunately, we cannot yet store it efficiently, so it has to be used as it is generated, and that needs a very efficient system for transmitting it around the country. We do this by means of the National Grid.

Increasingly, alternative sources of electrical energy are being sought to supplement that being obtained from nuclear or fossil fuel generators. These include wind energy, direct solar energy, wave energy, tidal energy and geothermal sources.

In capturing this energy, most systems use a simple principle. The movement of air or water is used to turn a **dynamo** which generates electricity. This principle has resulted in some complicated and interesting engineering. The photograph on the left shows a wind energy conversion system on the Orkney Islands which feeds electricity directly into the island grid and provides three million watts of power. A good way to understand the use of wind energy is to build a model and find out how well it performs.

## Activities

1. You are going to try to model a horizontal wind-energy conversion system.
   Try to design a simple flat vane system. Here are some questions you should consider:
   i) How many vanes are you going to use? (Two? three? four? six?)
   ii) How will you attach the vanes to the horizontal axle? You will need a hub of some sort.
   iii) How will you attach the vanes to the spokes?
   iv) What materials will you use for the hub, vanes and spokes?
   v) What shape and size will you make the vanes?
   vi) How will you support the axle? What sort of bearings could you use?
   vii) How will you prevent the axle from slipping out?
   viii) What structure will you use to hold the axle–vane assembly in the wind?

2. After building it you have to test the model. Hold the model in a light breeze. If you are indoors use a vacuum cleaner on 'blow'. Do the vanes turn? Adjust the angle of the vanes until you get the fastest speed or rotation.
   To measure the power of the model you need to measure the amount of work it can do in a given time. Use string on the horizontal axle to lift a weight and find the maximum weight your model can lift for a given wind speed. Measure this weight in **newtons** (N). Time how long it takes to lift this weight through 1 metre.

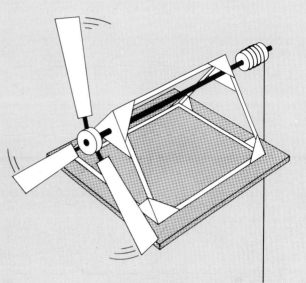

*Example* – If a model lifts 0.5 N through 1 m it does $0.5 \times 1$ N m of work. This equals 0.5 **joules** of work.

[Work done (joules) = Force (N) × Distance (m).]

If the model does this work in 5 seconds the power is given by work done divided by the time taken to do it:

Power = 0.5 J 5 sec
= 0.1 J/sec
= 0.1 watts

Is your model more powerful than this?
How does the power depend on wind speed?
Is there a relationship between speed of rotation and power output?
Can you modify your model to improve its performance?

### Energy conservation

It is important not to waste energy. Many industrial processes use heat, and we have to keep ourselves and our surroundings warm. The consequences of failing to do this can be fatal. The use of materials and systems that reduce waste and other sources of heat loss have become important parts of designing. Look back at the Materials section to find out which materials have low thermal conductivity and might be useful for preventing heat loss.

## Activity

Analyse the energy use in a fast-food outlet. How can you minimise the energy used for heating and cooling, and how might you use 'waste' heat from both?
Draw a card surface development to model take-away cartons for a range of fast foods. To reduce heat loss you should try to minimise the surface area compared to the volume.

# Systems

All systems have one thing in common: they are formed from different parts that **interact** in some organised way. Consider the system that supplies us with fresh water. It consists of a never-ending cycle of evaporation/transpiration and rainfall.

Look at the scene shown above. It illustrates the basic components of the **hydrological cycle**. The cycle is actually very complex, but it is often useful to show such complex systems as simple **block diagrams** like this.

Another type of system diagram can be used to model a motor car engine. Here a highly complex process is broken down into three elements: **inputs**, **processes** and **outputs**. Think how helpful this type of diagram would be in representing other complex systems, like an oil refinery!

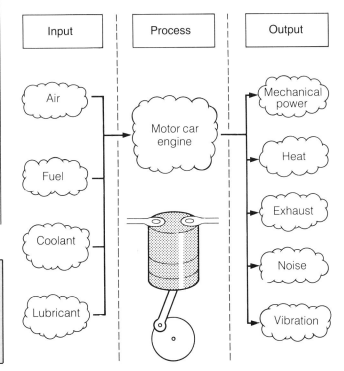

## Activities

1. Try and think of another natural system and draw a diagram to illustrate its operation.

2. Identify and draw a system known to you that has obvious inputs, processes and outputs.

## Interactive systems

As I type the text for this book onto a word processor, I am interacting with quite a complex system – more complex than most of the other systems that you have looked at so far.

As I type, I am looking at the text as it appears on the screen and making decisions as to how well it reads. If I am not satisfied with it or I make a mistake it is easy to change.

I am constantly monitoring what I am typing, and perhaps changing the structure of the text as I progress. I am applying what is known as a **feedback loop** to the system. The system (me, the keyboard, the processor and the screen) is interactive, and the feedback enables the system to function efficiently.

Many natural systems have some form of built-in feedback. An interesting experiment would be to observe a large number of rabbits and foxes together, and to record how they survive over a relatively long period of time.

The graph illustrates how the foxes would eat the rabbits and thrive. Unfortunately, the rabbits would soon decline and reduce the food for the foxes! Inevitably then, the fox population will decline as their food supply disappears. As there are now fewer foxes eating the rabbits the rabbits will start to become more abundant, and so the cycle repeats itself.

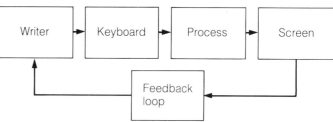

Natural systems have negative feedback

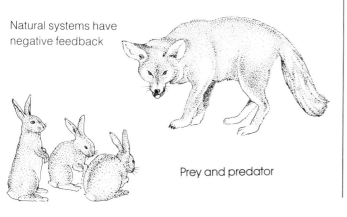

Prey and predator

This type of feedback is known as **negative feedback**, as it tends to oppose the system's change. There is also a time delay in this system, so it is said to be **oscillating**.

Understanding systems is vital to the work we shall be doing later in the control section.

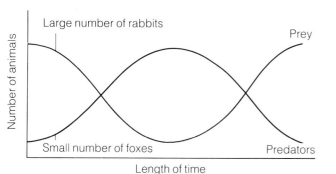

(Graph illustrates how prey and predators interact over a long period of time)

## Activities

1. Discuss with a friend a system that is familiar to you and try to identify any negative feedback loops that might exist in it. Draw a diagram of the system you have chosen, showing the feedback loops where possible.

2. Take a simple task, like frying an egg. Represent it as a systems diagram and identify the sources of feedback and how they enable you to keep control of the activity.

Controlling something involves two things. Firstly, **achieving** a given condition and, secondly, **maintaining** that condition.

It is often relatively simple to meet the first condition. For example, consider a simple circuit for dimming a lamp. This is known as **open loop** control, as there is no automatic way of maintaining the set brightness of the lamp as the battery voltage falls.

To meet the second condition you must apply some form of negative feedback to the system. A simple example of this can be seen in the control valve which maintains the water level in the tank in your loft.

Simple closed loop control system

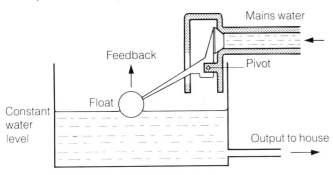

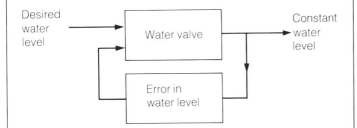

A simplified diagram of a toaster

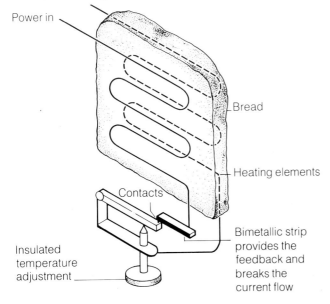

Simple open loop control (no feedback)

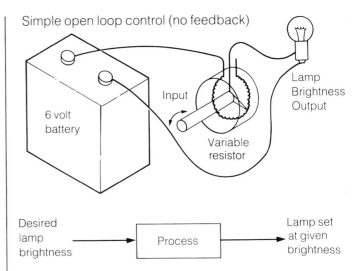

Can you see how the flow is shut off by the valve as the water level rises? The feedback is achieved through the float being connected to the valve in such a way as to shut the water off as the float rises. This is an example of **closed loop** control with negative feedback. How would you alter the water level in the tank?

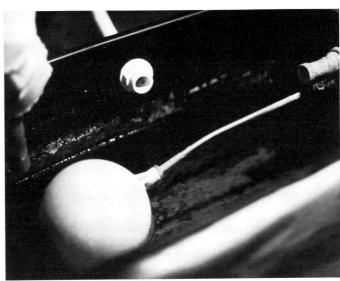

Another example of closed loop control can be observed in the way that a domestic toaster operates. Put the bread in and wait for it to be toasted is the theory – but we all know that toasters often produce unpredictable results.

### So what's going wrong with the control system?
There are many different types of bread – large or small slices, or perhaps bread straight from the freezer. In theory the toaster should cope with all these variables if it has true closed-loop negative feedback, but most systems are compromises between cost and efficiency. If you wanted a toaster that catered for every possibility it would end up a very much more complex (and costly) item than you are used to.

The automatic washing machine has a number of systems which are far more complex than the toaster, and what's more they all interact during the washing activity. How, for example, is the water level controlled in a typical machine?

As you will see from the diagram, the weight of the water is used to compress air. This pressure acts on a large rubber diaphragm which produces enough force to operate a microswitch. This is used to activate a solenoid-operated water valve. If a ball-cock valve had been used (like in the water tank) you can see that it would repeatedly bob up and down, switching the water on and off as the machine washed the clothes. The pressure-operated system is not so sensitive to the slopping water as it is the **average** pressure that controls the water valve.

Another important feature of this system is the 'damping' effect of the column of water and pressurised air that operates on the diaphragm. This damping effectively smooths out the dynamic action in the system and makes it much more stable. Without some form of damping, many systems would become unstable and break into uncontrolled oscillation (hunting).

The last system we shall look at is the remote-control link used for a television set. This is usually based on an infra-red beam. It is switched on and off very rapidly to form coded sequences of pulses that the receiver recognises as unique codes.

Depending on which code is sent, the receiver changes the channel or alters the volume level. Where is the feedback in this system?

Control system for an automatic washer

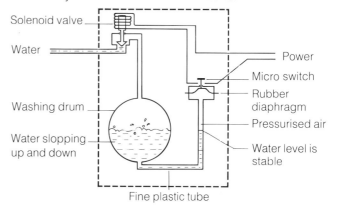

Infra-red control system

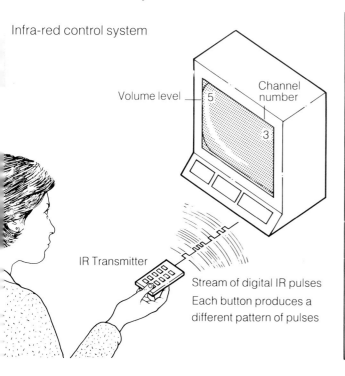

IR Transmitter

Stream of digital IR pulses
Each button produces a different pattern of pulses

## Activities

1. Make a list of the control systems you can identify in your home.

2. Look at the central heating system in your house or in a friend's house. Try to identify what the inputs to the system are, what the outputs are and how the control of the system is achieved. Produce a neat diagram illustrating the inputs, outputs and feedback loops.

3. Look carefully at how the 'damping' effect is achieved in the water-level control of the automatic washing machine. How might this damping effect be increased to make the switching even more stable?

4. Think about how a person interacts with the television remote-control system. How is the feedback loop formed? Draw a diagram of the system.

Electronics is an enormously versatile and effective means of establishing control within systems. The variety of circuit designs that can be used for any particular task is enormous. To illustrate this point we shall investigate a number of possible solutions to the following design brief.

An anemometer head is fixed to the roof of a school building. Design a device that will display the wind velocity in the geography room, which is two floors below.

A group of pupils attempted this problem in the Thames TV programme *"Using Microelectronics"*.

THAMES

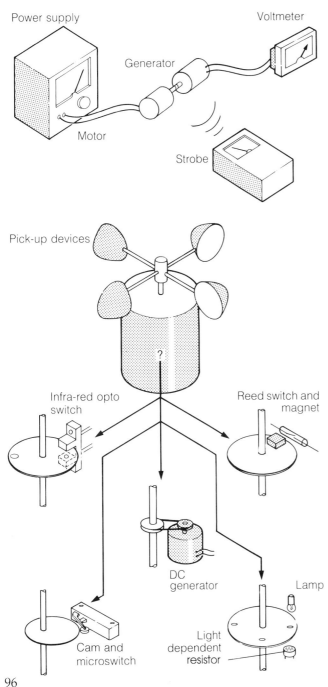

Power supply

Voltmeter

Generator

Motor

Strobe

Pick-up devices

Infra-red opto switch

Reed switch and magnet

DC generator

Lamp

Cam and microswitch

Light dependent resistor

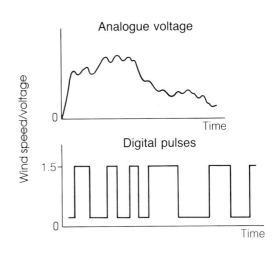

Analogue voltage

Wind speed/voltage

0

Time

Digital pulses

1.5

0

Time

## What options do you have?

There are two basic ways that electronic signals can be processed.

1. You could use a DC **analogue** voltage that is related to the speed of rotation.

2. The second method would be to pick up a number of **digital** pulses for every turn of the head.

The advantage of using a DC voltage to represent rotational speed is that it will not require much processing. A simple voltmeter will do. You could investigate how well this would work by connecting the shafts of two small electric motors together with a short length of plastic tube. A variable-voltage power supply could then be used to power one motor and a voltmeter connected to the other motor would indicate the voltage output. The speed of rotation could be measured with a stroboscope, and you could plot your results on a graph.

## How efficient is this system?

Unfortunately, the generator will require a considerable amount of energy to drive it, and the anemometer will therefore be insensitive to low wind speeds. Also, the voltage output will not be linear over its entire range.

By contrast, digital pulses will require more processing, but offer greater accuracy and flexibility in displaying the wind velocity.

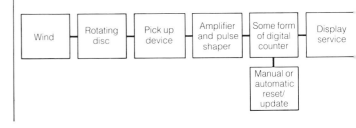

| Wind | Rotating disc | Pick up device | Amplifier and pulse shaper | Some form of digital counter | Display service |

Manual or automatic reset/ update

## Digital solutions

The simplest digital system that can be assembled is made up of a microswitch, an electro-mechanical counter and a battery. However, as the system is electro-mechanical, there are limits on how fast the counter can work. Also, operating the microswitch will add friction to the turning of the anemometer head.

The microswitch will also produce what is called 'bounce'. This is where the contacts do not open and shut cleanly – they in fact oscillate much as a ball does if it is dropped on a solid floor. This does not really matter to the electro-mechanical counter, as it is too slow to respond. But, unfortunately, an electronic counter would be able to count all the oscillations as well! Therefore, we must look for a different pick-up method.

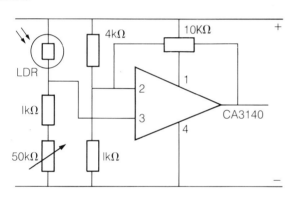

Display devices

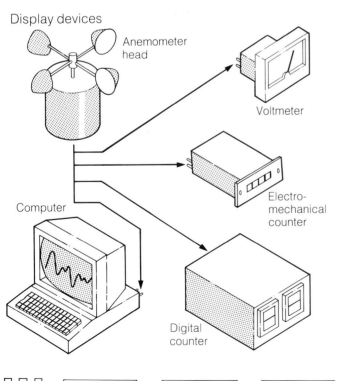

Anemometer head

Voltmeter

Electro-mechanical counter

Computer

Digital counter

Shaped pulses from anenometer head

Input/output port — Digital computer — VDU

Software (machine code) — Dot matrix printer

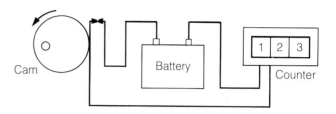

Cam    Battery    Counter

Consider the light-dependent resistor and lamp. This method is capable of producing single changes of resistance as the light falls on and off it, but, if these changes in resistance are plotted out, they do not appear in a clear 'square-sided' form. And, unfortunately, digital-counter chips require very sharp edges to the input pulses to work effectively.

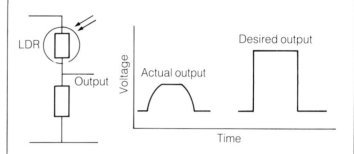

LDR    Output    Voltage    Actual output    Desired output    Time

What we need is some form of amplifier that is capable of shaping the pulses before they are counted. The CA3140 is an ideal microchip that can be set up as a comparator with some feedback.

You can see from the diagram that there is also a variable resistor, so that the sensitivity of the circuit can be adjusted. The output from this circuit can be fed directly to a digital counter or computer input/output (I/O) port.

Digital counters can be easily constructed from CMOS chips, seven segment displays and plug-in 'breadboards'. Manufacturers' data books will supply you with the necessary details.

If you can program a computer in Basic or, better still, Assembler, the simplest system to implement is one in which the output from the pulse-shaper is fed directly into the I/O port of the computer. It is then possible to process and display the information gathered from the anemometer head in a great variety of ways.

## Activity

Two pick-up devices shown in the diagram have not been discussed here as possibilities for using in the design of the system described above. Find out about them, and discover how they could be used.

Computers can be used for an enormous range of acitvities by just changing the controlling program. Some of these uses are listed below.

1. Computer-assisted learning (CAL)
2. Computer-aided design (CAD)
3. Word processing
4. Data processing
5. Program development
6. System modelling
7. Computer control

## THE BBC MICROBE COMPUTER

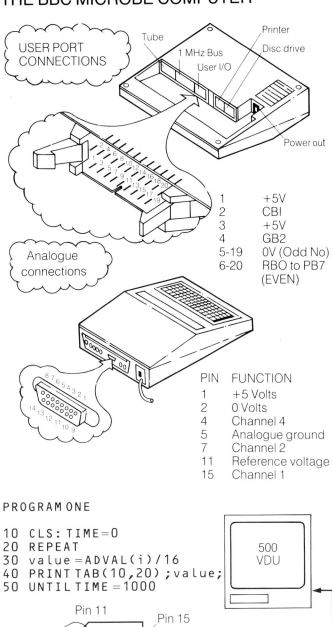

| | |
|---|---|
| 1 | +5V |
| 2 | CBI |
| 3 | +5V |
| 4 | GB2 |
| 5-19 | 0V (Odd No) |
| 6-20 | RBO to PB7 (EVEN) |

| PIN | FUNCTION |
|---|---|
| 1 | +5 Volts |
| 2 | 0 Volts |
| 4 | Channel 4 |
| 5 | Analogue ground |
| 7 | Channel 2 |
| 11 | Reference voltage |
| 15 | Channel 1 |

```
PROGRAM ONE

10  CLS: TIME=0
20  REPEAT
30  value =ADVAL(i)/16
40  PRINT TAB(10,20);value;
50  UNTIL TIME=1000
```

Pin 11
Pin 15
500 VDU
BBC 'B' Computer
Pin 5
Analogue port
Channel 1

It is this flexibility that makes microcomputers such powerful devices. These two pages will concentrate on using the BBC 'B' micro for control applications. The 'Beeb' is a particularly good machine for controlling external devices. It has a four channel analogue port and an eight bit I/O port which can be configured as eight bits out, eight bits in or any combination of these. The printer port can also be used as an eight bit output channel.

A WORD OF WARNING These ports can be damaged by excessive currents or voltages. It is best to use an **interface** that isolates the micro from your circuitry. Some exciting things can be achieved once you understand the principles involved.

### Analogue signals

We live in a world of **analogue systems**. The room temperature moves up and down by subtle degrees, passing traffic gets noisier or quieter through gradual increments. If you are to use computers for control applications in this analogue world, you must first see how analogue signals can be entered into the machine. If a voltage between 0 and 1.8 is fed into channel 1 of the analogue port, the Beeb will convert it into a number between 0 and 4095. The command value, ADVAL(1)/16, will return this number into the store 'value'. A simple variable resistor will produce a voltage that is proportional to the setting of the shaft. Type the program in and connect the potentiometer and try it.

```
PROGRAM ONE
10   CLS:TIME = 0
20   REPEAT
30   value = ADVAL(1)/16
40   PRINT TAB(10,20); value; ' '
50   UNTIL TIME = 1000
```

Light and temperature levels can also be converted into a voltage and fed into the analogue port. It is interesting to display these in a graphical form. The following program will achieve this.

```
PROGRAM TWO
10   MODE 0: X=0
20   REPEAT
30   y=ADVAL(1)/64
40   PLOT 5,x,y
50   x=x+1
60   UNTIL x> 1279
```

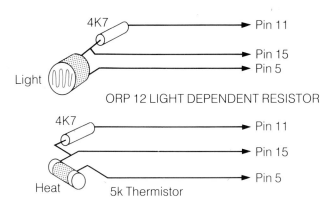

4K7 → Pin 11
→ Pin 15
→ Pin 5
Light

ORP 12 LIGHT DEPENDENT RESISTOR

4K7 → Pin 11
→ Pin 15
→ Pin 5
Heat
5k Thermistor

You should remember when using light-dependent resistors (LDRs) and thermistors that their characteristics are non-linear.

Analogue signals are very useful sources of data in any control system. Unfortunately, the conversion into digital codes is a rather slow process. An alternative approach is to use the I/O port for the input or output of digital pulses. This port can operate at very high transfer rates when the computer is programmed in machine code. Simple light-emitting diodes (LEDs) and relays can be switched with the two circuits below.

470Ω
I/O Port
3k9
BC183

5V Contacts to drive external circuit
I/O Port
10k
5V Relay
BC183
BFY51

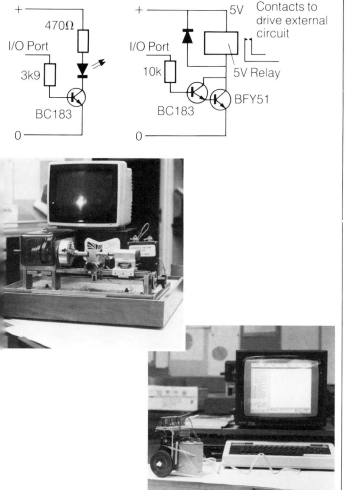

The buggy has its own battery supply. This power is switched to each of the two motors by a combination of three relays. Two of them switch either motor on or off and the third reverses the direction of either motor. The relays are controlled by computer software switching the I/O port. You can imagine that the buggy can be driven about by switching the appropriate relay.

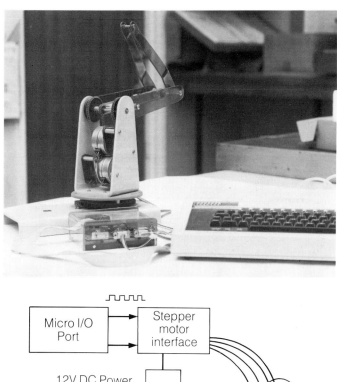

Micro I/O Port → Stepper motor interface
12V DC Power supply

Controlling stepper motors

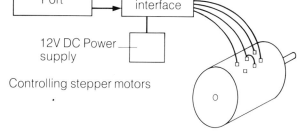

### What type of control is this?

There is no way that the computer can know how far the buggy actually travelled, as there is no feedback. So this is open loop control.

A better system can be assembled using the motor, gears and opto-sensor shown opposite. You can imagine how the sensor could feed pulses back into the computer port. These would relate directly to how far the motor had rotated.

Another method of controlling movement is to use a stepper motor. These very useful devices respond to certain patterns of pulses sent to them from a special driver chip. All the micro has to do is to switch one of the I/O outputs on and off 48 times for every revolution required. The direction of rotation is also controlled with one output switched on or off.

Both the lathe and the robot arm are driven with stepper motors connected to the micro.

All technology syllabuses establish a base line – or common core – of technological material. Most Examination Groups (NEA is the exception) thereafter take a **modular** approach in the development of their syllabus. This means that teachers and pupils can afford to be more selective and specific in the ground that they choose to cover in depth. The disadvantage of this, of course, is that in studying the details of the modules, one can lose sight of how they can all combine in the solution of technological problems. One way around this problem lies in the **systems** approach developed by the NEA. This checklist is therefore in three parts.

   i)  typical **common core** content in technology,
  ii)  the non-modular **systems** approach,
 iii)  typical technology **modules**.

## i) Common Core areas

1. **Designing, making and evaluating**
   In all syllabuses, you will be expected to understand and be able to operate as a designer in the ways outlined in the first section of this book. This means being able to:
   - identify design problems
   - investigate problems
   - generate and develop solutions
   - communicate ideas through 2D sketching and drawing, and through 3D modelling techniques
   - make prototype solution using workshop techniques
   - evaluate solutions.

2. **Materials**
   Classification, sources, description, properties and selection.

3. **Energy**
   Sources, forms, conversion and conservation.

4. **Control**
   Elements of systems – feedback, electronic, mechanical and pneumatic devices.

5. **Technology and society**
   History of technology, communications, automation, environment, values in a technological society, social, economic and political influences and the individual and society.

### ii) The systems approach

As you saw on pages 92–93, a system has three elements: input, process and output.

If technological problems are tackled by seeing them as a part of a system, then studying one particular area of knowledge (a module) is not particularly helpful. The systems approach builds on the common core areas of **materials**, **energy**, **control** and **technology in society**, and helps you to develop the knowledge you need to tackle that problem. This approach is therefore project-based.

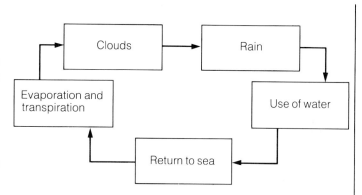

### iii) Typical modules

#### 1. Electronics
Current, voltage, Ohm's Law, AC/DC, resistors, capacitors, diodes, circuits, testing of circuits, storage of energy, switches, transistors as switches and as amplifiers, oscilloscopes, light and heat sensing, delay, multivibrators, op-amps and interface devices.

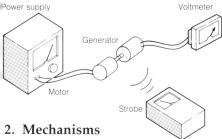

#### 2. Mechanisms
Load, effort, MA, VR, efficiency, motion, levers and linkages, transmission, pulleys and belts, sprockets and chains, gears, rack and pinion, cams, ratchet and pawl, clutches and brakes, bearings and lubrication and screws.

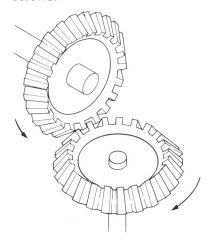

#### 3. Materials
Classification, properties, selection via properties, testing of properties, structures, sources, processing, composites and conservation.

#### 4. Structures
Types of structure, loads and reactions, turning forces, members, frames, materials, forces, joints, beams and testing of structures.

#### 5. Pneumatics
Compressors, linear motion, single- and double-acting cylinders, restrictors, detection of components, time delay, oscillation, automatic control, sequential control and fluids.

#### 6. Digital microelectronics
Current and voltage, analogue and digital, transistors as switches, logic gates, flipflops, Schmitt triggers, clocks, counting, microcomputers and computer control.

#### 7. Microprocessor Control
Microcomputers, digital information, decimal and hexadecimal notation, memory, input and output of signals, interfaces, Schmitt triggers, analogue and digital converters, control of machines, speed control and position sensing.

#### 8. Instrumentation
Measuring systems, electronic systems, signal production and processing, analogue and digital systems, transducers, counters and displays.

# Examination Checklist

These tables are a rough guide to the structure of the examination requirements for the five Examining Groups. The table shows the number and type of written papers, and the importance and timing of coursework. You should ask your teacher for more precise details of the particular course that you are doing.

| | | % | Term 1 | Term 2 | Term 3 | Term 4 | Term 5 | June exams |
|---|---|---|---|---|---|---|---|---|
| **LONDON AND EAST ANGLIAN GROUP** | | | | | | | | Pre-exam and 2 hrs |
| Paper 1 | Design | 20 | | | | | | |
| Paper 2 | Written exam  Part 1 – Common core  Part 2 – Modules | 30 | | | | | | 2½ hrs |
| Paper 3 | Project | 50 | | | | ←——————→ | | 45 hrs |
| **MIDLAND EXAMINING GROUP** | | | | | | | | Pre-exam and 2½ hrs |
| Paper 1 | Design | 20 | | | | | | |
| Paper 2 | Written exam – Common core | 10 | | | | | | 40 mins |
| Paper 3 | Written exam – Modules | 20 | | | | | | 1hr 20 mins |
| Projects | | 50 | | | | ←——————→ | | 40 hrs |
| **NORTHERN EXAMINING ASSOCIATION** | | | | | | | | |
| Paper 1 | Written exam – Short questions | 25 | | | | | | 1½ hrs |
| Paper 2 | Written exam – Technological problem solving | 25 | | | | | | 1½ hrs |
| Project | | 50 | | | | ←——————→ | | 45 hrs |
| **SOUTHERN EXAMINING GROUP** | | | | | | | | |
| Paper 1 | Written exam – Common core | 20 | | | | | | 1½ hrs |
| Paper 2 | Written exam – Modules | 30 | | | | | | 2 hrs |
| Projects | | 50 | | | | ←——————→ | | 45 hrs |
| **WELSH JOINT EDUCATION COMMITTEE** | | | | | | | | |
| Paper 1 | Written exam – Common core | 20 | | | | | | 1½ hrs |
| Paper 2 | Written exam – Modules | 30 | | | | | | 3 hrs |
| Mini projects | | 20 | ←——————————————→ | | | | | |
| Major projects | | 30 | | | | ←——————→ | | |

# *References*

This is a list of books which we think may be useful references for you on your CDT course. Remember also that there are many videos, TV programmes and magazines that you might find very helpful. Our list has the book title, author or editor, and publisher. We have also indicated in which part of the course they might be most useful.

## Common Core

*British Design since 1880*, MacCarthy, Lund Humphries
*CDT Foundation Course*, Finney & Fowler, Collins
*CDT Projects and Approaches*, Barlex and Kimbell, MacMillan
*Design, Designing, Engineering*, magazines, Design Council
*Design Matters*, Mayall, Design Council
*How Things Don't Work*, Papanek & Hennessey, Pantheon
*How Things Work*, Books 1 & 2, Paladin
*Introducing CDT*, Breckon & Prest, Thames/Hutchinson
*In Good Shape*, Bayley, Design Council
*Objects of Desire*, Forty, Thames and Hudson

## CDT: Design and Communication

*Introducing Design and Communication*, Tufnell, Hutchinson
*Manual of Graphic Techniques 1*, Porter & Greenstreet, Astragal
*Manual of Graphic Techniques 2, 3 & 4*, Porter & Goodman, Astragal
*The Alternative Printing Handbook*, Treweek, Penguin

## CDT: Design and Realisation

*Design and Craft*, Yarwood and Dunn, Hodder & Stoughton
*Design and Realisation*, Marden, Oxford University Press

## CDT: Technology

*Design and Technology*, Yarwood and Orme, Hodder & Stoughton
*Schools Council Modular Courses in Technology*, Oliver & Boyd

## Special Interest

*Aids for the Severeley Handicapped*, Copeland, Sector Publishing (Design for Disabled People)
*Body Space*, Pheasant, Taylor and Francis (Ergonomics)
*Computer Graphics*, Hearn & Baker, Prentice Hall (Computers)
*DIY Robotics and Sensors with the BBC*, Billingsley, Sunshine (Computers)
*Fun Furniture*, Sylvester, Windward (furniture)
*Housing Adaptations for Disabled People*, Lockhart, Architectural Press (Design for Disabled People)
*Human Dimensions and Interior Space*, Panero & Zelnik, Architectural Press (Ergonomics)
*Living by Design*, Gorlo (ed), Lund Humphries (Corporate Identity, Packaging, Information Design and Display)
*Making Small Wooden Boxes*, Jacobson, Sterling (Containers)
*Memphis*, Radice, Thames and Hudson (Furniture)
*On Camera*, Watts, BBC Publications (Cameras Film & Video)
*Paper Engineering*, Hiner, Tarquin Publications (Pop-up Books)
*Performing Wooden Toys*, Wells, Batsford (Toys)
*The House Book*, Conran, Mitchell Beazley (Interior)
*The Robot Book*, Pawson, Windward (Robots)
*The Small Garden*, Brookes, Cavendish Books (Exteriors)
*Townscape*, Cullen, Architectural Press (Exteriors)
*Vibrations-Making Unorthodox Musical Instruments*, Sawyer, Cambridge University Press (Music)
*Working Wooden Toys*, Millet, Link House (Toys)
*Your Cartoon Time*, Harris, Knight Books (Cartoons)

# Index